# A Witches Book of Shadows

# A Witches Book of Shadows

## Spells, Rituals, Sabbats and Journal Grimoire

### D.E. LUET

Publisher: A Witch Alone Publishing

ISBN (Paperback): 978-1-7773189-0-1

ISBN (Hardcover): 978-1-7773189-2-5

ISBN (eBook): 978-1-7773189-1-8

DISCLAIMER: The author of this book does not dispense medical advice or prescribe the use of any technique as a form of treatment for physical, emotional, or medical problems. The intent of the author is only to offer information of a general nature to help you in your quest for emotional and spiritual well-being. In the event, you use any of the information in this book, which is your constitutional right, the author and the publisher assume no responsibility for your actions.

Thank you.

To all of you that have followed me on my journey, and allowed me to be there for all of yours.

Let's continue together.

# Table of Contents

# Book of Shadows Blessing

Inside these pages you will find,
Wisdom from my heart and mind.
Knowledge passed not through words,
but energy and thoughts unheard.

From working with the moons bright glow,
To learning what my ancestors show,
Channeling Water, Fire, Air and Earth
My power flows and comes to birth

This text I will hold sacred and dear
Let no negativity ever enter near
I'll keep safe the secrets of old ways
Until I choose them to see the day

## This BoS Belongs To

# Using Your BoS

What you have in your hands, is not meant to be your first and only BOS or Grimoire. (If it ends up being that for you, then I'm glad!) What this is, is something to get you started, and to make preparing for your first spells, Sabbats, and daily practice a little easier.

When I first started on my path, I had no idea what to put in a BOS or where to start looking for what herbs did what or what colours meant what, it can be pretty overwhelming. How do you know if you have all of the information? How do you know if what you're reading is accurate?

Not only do you have pages upon pages of blank space to create your own BOS, but a mini Grimoire as well, in one convenient, easy to take with you or keep secret, package. You'll find pages of correspondences, pointers on how to create your own spells, and how to get into the groove of using your magic anywhere and everywhere. Practice makes progress. The more you can practice your craft, the more you'll progress in it, and the easier it will be to feel at home within your own power.

Most importantly, make this book your own. Grab your pencil crayons, highlighters, and markers. Get colourful pens, or stick with black. Get stickers. Doodle all over it, or keep it pristine. You are unique, your BOS should be too!

# What's Inside

## Blank Formatted Pages

Pages that have been organized to help you prepare for your working, or to help you remember what you did at the time! There is space for writing down astrological timing, deity work, ingredients, divination, meditation and your work space set up. There's also two sets of blank divination pages: one for small spreads like one or three card pulls, and one for larger spreads with ample room to draw out where the cards were positioned.

## Inventory List

A set of blank list pages where you can keep track of items that you've run out of and need to stock up on: crystals, herbs, incense, jars etc.

## Correspondences Tables

You have at your disposal, correspondence lists with some of the most basic but most asked about uses. Colours, herbs, crystals, moon phases, monthly moons, zodiac and Sabbats. Including blank sections to add in your most used and preferred ingredients. These pages also include tips like how to pick your crystals and harvesting your herbs safely and energetically friendly.

## Help

At the beginning of each section, you'll find a small blurb with tips in creating your own spells, modifying pre-constructed rituals, and making your own divination spreads. On top of that, there will be sample spells and rituals from my own personal Book of Shadows, to help you get started.

# SPELLS

# Spellwork

Creating your own spells can sound daunting, but it's really not that hard! In the back of the book you'll find everything you need to create a spell for some of the most common issues and intentions out there: good luck, abundance, love and more.

You don't need **every** ingredient on the list to make a spell work! You can use one, three, or ten ingredients if it makes you feel better. Ingredients can include herbs, crystals, the time of the day, the day of the week, a certain Sabbat, or a specific moon phase! Lots of ingredients make up a spell.

These pages can help you plan a spell ahead of time, or be there when you're in the middle of your spell and choose to change a word or phrase half way through! I encourage you to always make spells your own. Pick and choose from different formats and ingredients, make them rhyme, or not. Make them formal, or informal. Exuberant, or simple. Your power is personal, your spells can be just as personal too.

On the next page, you'll find the spellcrafting basics, basically a checklist for how to put together your own spell. What it comes down to is *who, what, where, when, why* and *how.* You might be thinking to yourself that some of these are pretty obvious, but you'd be surprised at what you don't know.

# Spellwork
## The Basics

**Who**—for the most part, if you're doing the spell for yourself than it is pretty obvious who your "who" is going to be. But if you're doing a spell for someone else, or *on* someone else, making sure your directing your energy to the right person is essential in success-ful spellwork. If you're finding it hard to concentrate as a new witch, try finding a photo of the person to focus on, but if you can't find that then simply write their name on a piece of paper. Keep these things on your altar or in your sacred space while you're performing the spell.

**What**—your "what" is going to be your spells ingredients, and this can be anything that is going to make up your spell. Physical ingredients like candles, herbs, crystals or incense. Do you need jars? Do you need sachets? Do you need a place to bury the spell or throw it to the wind?

**Where**—if you have a sacred space or an altar, your "where" is going to be pretty straightforward as well. If you're practicing in the broom closet, you may need to change your "where" every time you try and practice. All I can say is that when choosing your "where", make sure of a few things: you are being safe, and you are grounding./cleansing the space before and after use.

**When**—the "when" is the metaphysical half of the "what". This is timing your spell for the utmost success. Is there a time of the day when it is going to be better? Moon phase? Weekday? Or maybe waiting until a Sabbat or a certain Zodiac phase. This isn't necessary, especially if you need the spell done NOW, but if you can plan, this is always fun to do!

**Why**—the "why" is something that requires complete and utter honesty with yourself. What is your true intention when it comes to your spell. Are you trying to attract the right lover to you because you're ready for a committed relationship, or because you want to make your ex jealous? Whatever your reason, own it honestly, or there's a chance your spell could backfire.

6

# Spellwork
## The Basics

<u>How</u>-your how is what method you're going to use to carry out your spell. Are you going to be carrying this with you or making a charm? Then a bottle or jar spell would be best. If you're doing a sleep spell, then a sachet would probably be the way to go so you aren't sleeping on something so rigid like a jar. For quick release and manifestations, candle spells might be the one for you. You also would have to figure out which candle to use so that it burns for the appropriate time. (NEVER LEAVE A BURNING CANDLE UNATTENDED). These are just some of the examples of different spell methods, and they vary depending on the type of spell, and the severity.

<u>Grounding/Cleansing/Protecting</u>-as mentioned in the "where" basic, you want to make sure you cleanse the area, ground your energies, and set up protective barriers, before taking on any kind of spell or ritual work. But what does this mean?

*Cleansing* the space gets rid of any energies that might muck up your spell, and believe it or not, even the most positive energies can have an adverse effect depending on your spells intentions. I find the most effective ways of cleansing are *smoke* and *sound*. The easiest way to use smoke to cleanse an area is probably incense. You can find them in various lengths which can shorten or prolong their burn time. (Even when it goes out, the space is still cleansed.) If you can't use smoke, sound is also a great way to cleanse a space. The vibrations of the music/instrument help to knock out the unwanted energy. The most common instrument for witches ot use, is a bell. Ring it methodically to cleanse.

*Grounding* is something you want to do, in order to centre yourself and ground your energy before taking on the energies of the spell you're about to perform. Grounding can be as simple as feeling the floor beneath your feet and picturing your excess energy, or maybe negative energy from the day, melt away into the floorboards. It can also be a quick meditation. The point is to become totally engrossed in what you are about to do with your spell.

# Spellwork
## The Basics

Setting up protection barriers will help keep out any unwanted energy, or beings, that might intervene and change up the methods and intentions of your spell work. This is usually random, and not like any ethereal bodies are out to get you. But this can also be targeted by another witch who does not want you to be successful in your spell work, something I personally find very rare.

Setting up protecting barriers can be done a few ways:

*Salt*—you can use salt to outline a circle around where you will be working your spell if you have the space. You can also place salt above door frame and window frames, on window ledges and on the floor of the door frame. Salt is an excellent protector, and is easy to acquire, as table salt works fine.

*Crystals*—You can use certain crystals and place them again, on windowsills, around the door, or around your work space in a circle. You can out them in each corner of the room or in each direction, or both. Common crystals that would be good for this would be selenite, clear quartz, and amethyst.

*Cast a Circle*—if you're a little more experienced, or have a really good imagination, you can probably create a circle or a cone of power form your minds eye. This uses your own personal power and intent to create a protective space for you to do your work. Essentially you would imagine light coming from your fingertip or wand, and turn in a circle clockwise until you're surrounded by a large hoola hoop of energy. That energy would then expand until you're standing in a huge, glowing hamster wheel. When you are done with your spell, you can then imagine the sphere decreasing back into the hoola hoop, and turn in a counter-clockwise direction in order to absorb your precious energy back into you.

I hope these tips help you prepare for your spells! On the next page, you'll find a spell directly from my personal Book of Shadows. Happy spell casting!

# Example Spell
## Demon Banishing

Now, I could have included one of the "more tame" spells from my BoS, but since I have been told by the intended spell recipient that this particular banishment spell worked really well I elected to include this instead.

More messages that I want to admit have been scared witches who think that either something has followed them home, found it's way into their life by accident or has been sent to them on purpose. The worst thing that can happen here is that the spell doesn't work, which obviously would defeat the whole purpose of doing it. **But**, that can also mean that maybe it's not a malevolent spirit bothering you in the first place.

The point of this spell was to create banishment jars that would be put above all the entranceways, both doors and windows. I found small jars that would fit on top of the trim, and figured out how much of each herb and crystal I would post likely need. I use very small crystals for these spells so I usually buy the long crystal necklaces and cut the string so that they fit in the jars easy and I don't have to worry about trying to cut or break a tumbled/polished stone.

When I am doing spell work that requires a little extra power, I call in the elements and pick a deity that I think would be interested in the spell work I am doing. At the time of doing this spell in 2017, I was practicing with the Nordic pantheon and so I chose Vali because he is the known as "The Avenger" and Vadir because he is the God of revenge and stealth.

For most of my candle spells, I feel the need to ask for extra power and simply trust in my own power and ingredients that I have chosen with intent to fulfill the spells purpose!

If you choose to duplicate/perform this spell, definitely modify it for your craft. Remove the elements, change the wording, or put in the deities you work with!

# Spell

Date: _____ Time: **Late evening** Sun Sign: _____

Weekday: **Friday** Moon Phase: **Waning 3%** Moon Sign: _____

## Spell

Set up alter. Smoke cleansed
myself and my space. Called in
the elements

*I call to the element of
(earth/air/fire/water) please
aid me in this spell by lend-
ing your (strength/wisdom/
courage/love)*

*I please humbly ask the Norse
God (Vali/Vidar) to lend me
your power. Help me to (avenge
my friend _____ and
bring peace of mind from the
demon that haunts here/seek
revenge on the demon that has
attached itself to _____)*

Place the herbs and crystals
into the vials . Meditate on
intention of the spell while
filling. Thank the Gods with
libations, dismiss elements,
close the circle.

## Ingredients/Materials

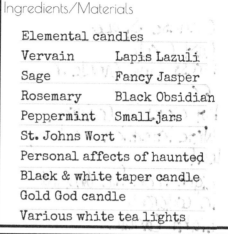

Elemental candles

Vervain          Lapis Lazuli

Sage             Fancy Jasper

Rosemary         Black Obsidian

Peppermint       Small jars

St. Johns Wort

Personal affects of haunted

Black & white taper candle

Gold God candle

Various white tea lights

## Deities/Spirits        Offerings
## Elements Invoked

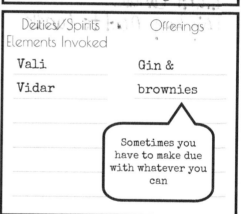

Vali             Gin &

Vidar            brownies

> Sometimes you
> have to make due
> with whatever you
> can

## Altar Set Up

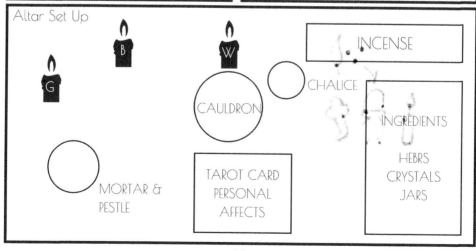

B

W

G

INCENSE

CHALICE

CAULDRON

INGREDIENTS

MORTAR &
PESTLE

TAROT CARD
PERSONAL
AFFECTS

HEBRS
CRYSTALS
JARS

# Spell

Date: **5/3**    Time: **8PM**    Sun Sign: **Taurus**
Weekday: **Wednesday** Moon Phase: **Wax. Gibbous** Moon Sign: **Libra**

## Spell

Cleanse Space
Cast Circle
Dress pink candle in
EO
Put cloves in couldron
Write intention on bay
leaf
Light it on fire and put
in couldron
Light Candle
Lay key next to candle

## Ingredients/Materials

Cloves
Sandalwood EO
~~Elemental Candles?~~
Pink candle
~~Pink Ribbon (if no candle)~~
Bay

## Deities/Spirits        Offerings
## Elements Invoked

Hecate                    key

## Altar Set Up

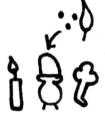

# Spell

Date: _____ Time: _____ Sun Sign:_____

Weekday:_____ Moon Phase: _____ Moon Sign:_____

## Spell

## Ingredients/Materials

## Deities/Spirits Elements Invoked

## Offerings

## Altar Set Up

# Spell

Date: _____ Time: _____ Sun Sign:_____

Weekday:_____ Moon Phase: _____ Moon Sign:_____

## Spell

## Ingredients/Materials

## Deities/Spirits Elements Invoked         Offerings

## Altar Set Up

# Spell

Date: _____ Time: _____ Sun Sign:_____

Weekday:_____ Moon Phase: _____ Moon Sign:_____

## Spell

## Ingredients/Materials

## Deities/Spirits
Elements Invoked

## Offerings

## Altar Set Up

# Spell

Date: _____ Time: _____ Sun Sign: _____

Weekday: _____ Moon Phase: _____ Moon Sign: _____

## Spell

## Ingredients/Materials

## Deities/Spirits          Offerings
Elements Invoked

## Altar Set Up

# Spell

Date: _____ Time: _____ Sun Sign:_____

Weekday:_____ Moon Phase: _____ Moon Sign:_____

## Spell

## Ingredients/Materials

## Deities/Spirits                Offerings
Elements Invoked

## Altar Set Up

# Spell

Date: _____ Time: _____ Sun Sign: _____

Weekday: _____ Moon Phase: _____ Moon Sign: _____

## Spell

## Ingredients/Materials

## Deities/Spirits       Offerings
## Elements Invoked

## Altar Set Up

# Spell

Date: _____ Time: _____ Sun Sign: _____

Weekday: _____ Moon Phase: _____ Moon Sign: _____

## Spell

## Ingredients/Materials

## Deities/Spirits          Offerings
## Elements Invoked

## Altar Set Up

# Spell

Date: _____ Time: _____ Sun Sign:_____

Weekday:_____ Moon Phase: _____ Moon Sign:_____

## Spell

## Ingredients/Materials

## Deities/Spirits          Offerings
Elements Invoked

## Altar Set Up

# Spell

Date: _____ Time: _____ Sun Sign:_____

Weekday:_____ Moon Phase: _____ Moon Sign:_____

## Spell

_____
_____
_____
_____
_____
_____
_____
_____
_____
_____
_____
_____
_____
_____
_____
_____
_____
_____
_____
_____

## Ingredients/Materials

_____
_____
_____
_____
_____
_____
_____
_____
_____
_____

## Deities/Spirits            Offerings
Elements Invoked

## Altar Set Up

# Spell

Date: _____ Time: _____ Sun Sign: _____

Weekday: _____ Moon Phase: _____ Moon Sign: _____

## Spell

## Ingredients/Materials

## Deities/Spirits
## Elements Invoked           Offerings

## Altar Set Up

# Spell

Date: _____ Time: _____ Sun Sign: _____

Weekday: _____ Moon Phase: _____ Moon Sign: _____

## Spell

## Ingredients/Materials

## Deities/Spirits        Offerings
Elements Invoked

## Altar Set Up

22

# Spell

Date: _____ Time: _____ Sun Sign: _____

Weekday: _____ Moon Phase: _____ Moon Sign: _____

## Spell

## Ingredients/Materials

## Deities/Spirits          Offerings
Elements Invoked

## Altar Set Up

# Spell

Date: _____ Time: _____ Sun Sign: _____

Weekday: _____ Moon Phase: _____ Moon Sign: _____

## Spell

## Ingredients/Materials

## Deities/Spirits
## Elements Invoked          Offerings

## Altar Set Up

# Spell

Date: _____ Time: _____ Sun Sign: _____

Weekday: _____ Moon Phase: _____ Moon Sign: _____

## Spell

## Ingredients/Materials

## Deities/Spirits Elements Invoked

## Offerings

## Altar Set Up

# Spell

Date: _____ Time: _____ Sun Sign: _____

Weekday: _____ Moon Phase: _____ Moon Sign: _____

## Spell

## Ingredients/Materials

## Deities/Spirits Elements Invoked

## Offerings

## Altar Set Up

# Spell

Date: _____ Time: _____ Sun Sign:_____

Weekday:_____ Moon Phase: _____ Moon Sign:_____

## Spell

## Ingredients/Materials

## Deities/Spirits          Offerings
Elements Invoked

## Altar Set Up

# Spell

Date: _____ Time: _____ Sun Sign:_____

Weekday:_____ Moon Phase: _____ Moon Sign:_____

## Spell

## Ingredients/Materials

## Deities/Spirits          Offerings
Elements Invoked

## Altar Set Up

# Spell

Date: _____ Time: _____ Sun Sign:_____

Weekday:_____ Moon Phase: _____ Moon Sign:_____

## Spell

## Ingredients/Materials

## Deities/Spirits Elements Invoked          Offerings

## Altar Set Up

# Spell

Date: _____ Time: _____ Sun Sign:_____

Weekday:_____ Moon Phase: _____ Moon Sign:_____

## Spell

## Ingredients/Materials

## Deities/Spirits          Offerings
Elements Invoked

## Altar Set Up

# Spell

Date: _____ Time: _____ Sun Sign:_____

Weekday:_____ Moon Phase: _____ Moon Sign:_____

### Spell

### Ingredients/Materials

### Deities/Spirits          Offerings
### Elements Invoked

### Altar Set Up

# Spell

Date: _____ Time: _____ Sun Sign: _____

Weekday: _____ Moon Phase: _____ Moon Sign: _____

## Spell

## Ingredients/Materials

## Deities/Spirits          Offerings
Elements Invoked

## Altar Set Up

# Spell

Date: _____ Time: _____ Sun Sign:_____

Weekday:_____ Moon Phase: _____ Moon Sign:_____

## Spell

_____
_____
_____
_____
_____
_____
_____
_____
_____
_____
_____
_____
_____
_____
_____
_____
_____
_____
_____

## Ingredients/Materials

_____
_____
_____
_____
_____
_____
_____
_____
_____

## Deities/Spirits        Offerings
## Elements Invoked

_____  _____
_____  _____
_____  _____
_____  _____
_____  _____
_____  _____

## Altar Set Up

# SABBATS

# Sabbat Rituals

There are eight Sabbats that can be celebrated year round: one at each solstice(2), one at each equinox(2), and four others in between. Not every witch celebrates all eight, some only celebrate the solstices and equinoxes, some don't celebrate any of them and simply move with the way the seasons change in their area. However you celebrate, here are some tips to help you get started.

The eight Sabbats in order starts with the witches new year Samhain, and continues with Yule, Imbolc, Ostara, Beltane, Litha(Midsummer), Lammas(Lughnasadh), and Mabon. In the back of the journal you'll find all the necessary information to help you along creating your own ritual for the changing of the seasons.

One of the things I think that is key to remember in creating your own ritual, is that you're celebrating the natural time passing of the earth and the seasons. Don't overthink it! Sometimes rituals can be super simple, and sometimes you may want them to be huge and exuberant. You can celebrate rituals with others too if you are lucky enough to have open friends, family, or practitioners close by!

Put your ritual together for what helps you feel connected to the earth and it's changes, and how you may be changing at the same time. I always feel very connected to my rituals when I keep this practice in mind!

# Sabbat Rituals

Some things you may want to consider for celebrating your rituals when it comes to planning ahead, is what kind of food and drink you would like to enjoy on the day of. Are you celebrating with others? Knowing your numbers is also key, especially when it comes to the food aspect. How much bread should you bake? Are you going to make a summer salad for Litha? How big should it be? How many Yule Log cakes should you make for how many people?

There is also the drinks. In every book I've ever read, they always have "cakes and ale" after rituals or spells. Well when I was celebrating at 15, I couldn't exactly have an alcoholic beverage. There are many non-alcoholic alternatives, and even gluten-free alternatives for the cakes part if you can't have gluten.

Really what it comes down to, is having an easy finger food, and a complimentary beverage to go with the Sabbat. (These are included in the Grimoire at the back of the journal.) This can range from small cakes, to muffins, to bars, and even home made ice cream. You can have wine, cider (alcoholic or not) and even water for your drink.

Don't be afraid to change it up from Sabbat to Sabbat, or to go outside the traditional libations.

# Sabbat Example

This Sabbat celebration example is actually one that hasn't yet been put into my BoS, as it is for this Samhain coming. That's right, the Blue Moon Samhain Celebration.

In order to put together this celebration, I looked at all the theme surrounding **Blue Full Moons** and **Samhain** specifically.

|  | Blue Moon | Samhain |
|---|---|---|
| Herbs | Patchouli, mugwort, nutmeg | Mugwort, rosemary, yarrow |
| Crystals | Obsidian, onyx | Obsidian, onyx |
| Power Flow | Release, remember | Release, renewal |
| Colours | Black, purple | Black, silver, orange |

So what I have put together is a 3-part ritual using the above correspondences:

## Ancestor Meditation

-making Samhain mediation oil, anointing a candle and meditation on messages from ancestors

## Ultra R&R Candle Spell

-ultimate **release** and **renew** after the last year (especially 2020.)

## Dream Divination

-before and after Sabbat sleep spreads

For this example, I won't be including an altar set up drawing

# Samhain

Date: **October 31**

Weekday: **Saturday**

Moon: **Full Moon in Taurus**    Sun In: **Scorpio**

## Desire/Intentions

Micro Full Moon, second full moon in October 2020, as well as being Samhain. Releasing the

negativity from the past year, remembering what we are thankful for an our ancestors,

activating a renewing energy and renewing our own power.

## Ingredients/Materials

- Black Taper Candles (2)
- 1 Silver Chime Candle
- 1 Purple Chime Candle
- Patchouli, Mugwort, & Rosemary
- Obsidian & Onyx chips (small)
- Obsidian OR Onyx tumbled
- crystal or crystal point
- Safflower Oil & 2oz glass jar
- Lighter
- Tarot/Oracle Deck of choice

## Deities/Spirits    Offerings
## Elements Invoked

If you choose to invoke your/certain deities for Samhain, make sure you are offering them something from the season. (Check the Grimoire for more info.)

If you are honoring your ancestors, I suggest getting a little bit of their favorite drink/food to put out.

## Workings

**Meditation Oil** – 2 tbsp. Safflower oil. 1 tsp yarrow. 1 tsp mugwort. 1 tsp rosemary. Crush herbs together, place in jar and cover with Safflower oil. Leave in sunlight for a week before use. OR heat oil in double boil, add herbs and simmer for 2-4 hours. When oil is ready (can be done days-weeks before Samhain.) anoint Purple chime candle. Set up ancestor honouring plates, light candle and meditate on any messages they may send you. Write down any thoughts or visions that come to you. You may also anoint yourself with the oil but do no ingest.

**Ultra R&R Candle Spell** – Get a small dish. Like the dish with the patchouli, rosemary, mugwort, obsidian and onyx chips. Place the silver chime candle in the centre of the dish. While you light the candle, think about everything you want to release from the last year. Physically, mentally, spiritually. Let the candle full burn out then bury everything in the Earth.

## Ancestor Message Spread

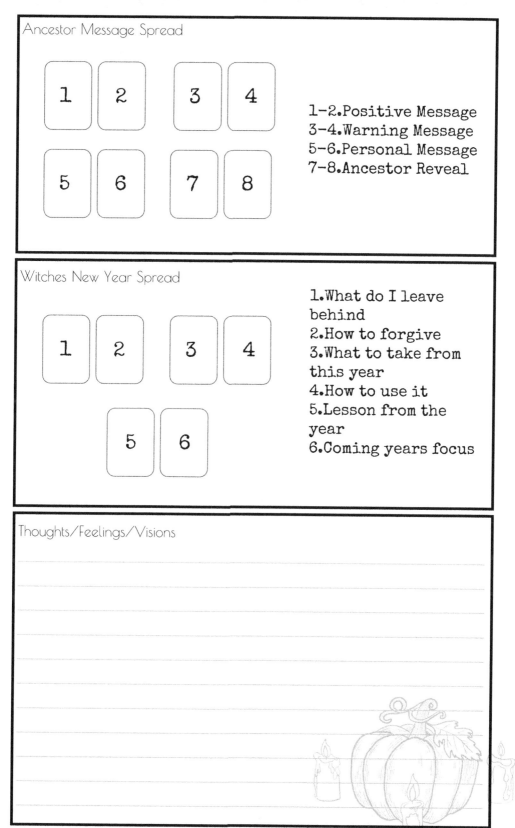

1
2
3
4

5
6
7
8

1-2.Positive Message
3-4.Warning Message
5-6.Personal Message
7-8.Ancestor Reveal

## Witches New Year Spread

1
2
3
4

5
6

1.What do I leave behind
2.How to forgive
3.What to take from this year
4.How to use it
5.Lesson from the year
6.Coming years focus

## Thoughts/Feelings/Visions

# Samhain

Date: _____ Weekday: _____

Moon Phase: _____

Moon Sign:_____Sun Sign: _____

## Desire/Intentions

## Ingredients/Materials

## Deities/Spirits
Elements Invoked

## Offerings

## Workings

Altar Set Up

Divination

Thoughts/Feelings/Visions

# Yule

Date: _____ Weekday: _____

Moon Phase: _____

Moon Sign: _____ Sun Sign: _____

## Desire/Intentions

## Ingredients/Materials

## Deities/Spirits          Offerings
Elements Invoked

## Workings

## Altar Set Up

## Divination

## Thoughts/Feelings/Visions

# Imbolc

Date: _____ Weekday: _____

Moon Phase: _____

Moon Sign:_____ Sun Sign: _____

## Desire/Intentions

## Ingredients/Materials

## Deities/Spirits          Offerings
Elements Invoked

## Workings

Altar Set Up

Divination

Thoughts/Feelings/Visions

# Ostara

Date: _____ Weekday: _____

Moon Phase: _____

Moon Sign:_____Sun Sign: _____

## Desire/Intentions

_____
_____
_____
_____

## Ingredients/Materials

_____
_____
_____
_____
_____
_____
_____
_____

## Deities/Spirits Elements Invoked     Offerings

## Workings

_____
_____
_____
_____
_____
_____
_____
_____
_____
_____

## Altar Set Up

## Divination

## Thoughts/Feelings/Visions

# Beltane

Date: _____ Weekday: _____

Moon Phase: _____

Moon Sign:_____ Sun Sign: _____

## Desire/Intentions

_____
_____
_____
_____

## Ingredients/Materials

_____
_____
_____
_____
_____
_____
_____
_____
_____

## Deities/Spirits Elements Invoked          Offerings

_____    _____
_____    _____
_____    _____
_____    _____
_____    _____
_____    _____
_____    _____

## Workings

_____
_____
_____
_____
_____
_____
_____
_____
_____
_____
_____
_____

Altar Set Up

Divination

Thoughts/Feelings/Visions

# Litha

Date: _____ Weekday: _____

Moon Phase: _____

Moon Sign:_____Sun Sign: _____

## Desire/Intentions

## Ingredients/Materials

## Deities/Spirits          Offerings
Elements Invoked

## Workings

## Altar Set Up

## Divination

## Thoughts/Feelings/Visions

# Lammas

Date: _____ Weekday: _____

Moon Phase: _____

Moon Sign: _____ Sun Sign: _____

## Desire/Intentions

## Ingredients/Materials

## Deities/Spirits
Elements Invoked

Offerings

## Workings

Altar Set Up

Divination

Thoughts/Feelings/Visions

# Mabon

Date: _____ Weekday: _____

Moon Phase: _____

Moon Sign: _____ Sun Sign: _____

## Desire/Intentions

## Ingredients/Materials

## Deities/Spirits    Offerings
Elements Invoked

## Workings

Altar Set Up

Divination

Thoughts/Feelings/Visions

# RITUALS

# Rituals

So what other rituals could you be doing besides Sabbats? Lots! If you practice with a certain pantheon of deities (a set of Gods and Goddesses.) and they have days specific to them where you wish to celebrate. 95% of deities have a day unto themselves, and therefore they have their own ways of which people used to celebrate them. Certain activities, games, foods and drinks for that day.

There is also rituals revolving around the moon phases. You can do a ritual for the major moon phases: full, waning, new and waxing, or just for one a month if putting together a ritual per phase seems daunting. You also don't *have* to do a ritual for every full moon of every month, or every new moon. Sometimes you will have intentions to set, and other times you will simply put out your crystals or decks to charge under its light.

Rituals can also be those of self-love: set some candles, connect with yourself, meditate, ground, do divination. They don't need to have an ulterior motive or to have some grand plan, they can just be what you need in order to center yourself. Maybe you've had a really stressful week and you're about to change your bathtub into an area of self-ritual. Witches need self-care too!

# Rituals

One thing I suggest, is to have a checklist of things you do before your rituals, similar to the grounding and cleansing of pre-spell work. This might change depending on what exactly you're doing for your ritual. For instance, maybe you have a specific incense you always light before getting down to full moon business. That incense wouldn't have the same effect on a new moon, or on a deity-specific celebration.

Pre-ritual baths are very common, as water is the element that coincides with cleansing. You're essentially preparing yourself to work your magic, by cleansing away any of the energy or thoughts or issues from the day/week/moon phase before hand. Not everyone likes baths. (I know, like what?) so maybe they have an herbal mist or a yoga flow that helps cleanse their energy.

But I'll remind you again, don't overthink it! If you're stressing about creating a ritual or making it perfect, maybe put the journal down. Read a book. Go for a walk. Breathe. Connect back with yourself and your original intention, and then come back to work your magic.

You have enough pages here for all of the full moons in a year, including the Blue Moon, as well as some extra pages!

# Ritual Example
New Moon for Success

So a lot of the times when I plan out my lunar rituals, I look at a few things:

-what is the power flow of this phase
-what zodiac sign is it in
-how can I use both of these

It doesn't always work out that the zodiac sign and the power flow match up, and that's okay. For this new moon, I was cultivating success for the book you are now holding in your hands! (Did it work? Haha). But because of the moon being in Leo, I actually ended up performing two spreads for myself.

So while my candle spell was to bring upon the success, my divination was a combination of my Lions Heart spread because of my desire to shed a little bit of light onto my own soul, and the 9 card spread that I have featured on the Ritual page.

Some witches might think this is a big no-no to mix intentions or though processes, but for me, I have 2 hours to let the candle burn to nothing and sometimes I want to experience the other sections of that lunar phase.

The important thing, as always, is to do what feels right for you and what *you* need at that time.

# Ritual

Date: __August 17, 2020__  Time: __8:30-ish pm__  Sun Sign: __Cancer__

Weekday: __Monday__  Moon Phase: __New__  Moon Sign: __Leo__

Occasion: __New Moon Ritual__  Weather: __Started w/clear skies, then turned to rain__

## Desire/Intentions

Using the energy of the new moon to manifest success with this new endeavor of the book. Not to get rich, but to be able to have a stable income to support family and be a stay at home mom.

## Ingredients/Materials

Brown chime candle
Garnet, Rose Quartz, Citrine
Chamomile, Yarrow, Vervain
Dish for burning
Lighter
Sandalwood Incense

## Deities/Spirits  Offerings
Elements Invoked

## Divination

|  | BODY | MIND | SOUL |
| --- | --- | --- | --- |
| PAST | | | |
| PRESENT | | | |
| FUTURE | | | |

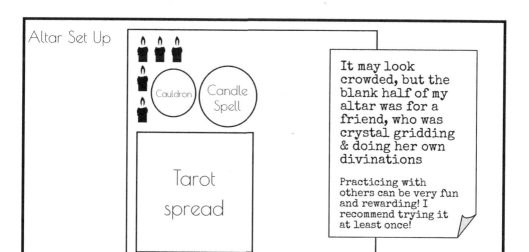

It may look crowded, but the blank half of my altar was for a friend, who was crystal gridding & doing her own divinations

Practicing with others can be very fun and rewarding! I recommend trying it at least once!

## Ritual/Spell

Light sandalwood incense

Line the dish with Garnet, Rose Quartz, Citrine, Chamomile, Yarrow, and Vervain

Place brown candle in the middle of dish

Light candle

Meditate on cultivating success through the hard work. It won't just drop into my lap but I am confident that if I work hard, that hard work will be seen and readily rewarded.

Let candle burn to nothing and bury spell in the Earth at the base of a very tall tree.

# Ritual

Date: _____ Time: _____ Sun Sign:_____

Weekday:_____ Moon Phase: _____ Moon Sign:_____

Occasion: _____ Weather:_____

Desire/Intentions

Ingredients/Materials

Deities/Spirits          Offerings
Elements Invoked

Divination

## Altar Set Up

## Ritual/Spell

# Ritual

Date: _____ Time: _____ Sun Sign:_____

Weekday:_____Moon Phase: _____ Moon Sign:_____

Occasion: _____Weather:_____

**Desire/Intentions**

_____
_____
_____

**Ingredients/Materials**

_____
_____
_____
_____
_____
_____

**Deities/Spirits          Offerings
Elements Invoked**

_____     _____
_____     _____
_____     _____
_____     _____
_____     _____

**Divination**

_____
_____
_____
_____
_____
_____
_____
_____
_____
_____

Altar Set Up

Ritual/Spell

# Ritual

Date: _____ Time: _____ Sun Sign:_____
Weekday:_____Moon Phase: _____ Moon Sign:_____
Occasion: _____Weather:_____

## Desire/Intentions

## Ingredients/Materials

## Deities/Spirits        Offerings
Elements Invoked

## Divination

Altar Set Up

Ritual/Spell

# Ritual

Date: _____ Time: _____ Sun Sign:_____

Weekday:_____Moon Phase: _____ Moon Sign:_____

Occasion: _____Weather:_____

## Desire/Intentions

## Ingredients/Materials

## Deities/Spirits
Elements Invoked          Offerings

## Divination

Altar Set Up

Ritual/Spell

# Ritual

Date: _____ Time: _____ Sun Sign:_____

Weekday:_____Moon Phase: _____ Moon Sign:_____

Occasion: _____Weather:_____

Desire/Intentions

Ingredients/Materials

Deities/Spirits          Offerings
Elements Invoked

Divination

Altar Set Up

Ritual/Spell

# Ritual

Date: _____ Time: _____ Sun Sign:_____

Weekday:_____ Moon Phase: _____ Moon Sign:_____

Occasion: _____ Weather:_____

## Desire/Intentions

_____

_____

_____

## Ingredients/Materials

_____

_____

_____

_____

_____

_____

_____

## Deities/Spirits    Offerings
Elements Invoked

## Divination

Altar Set Up

Ritual/Spell

# Ritual

Date: _____ Time: _____ Sun Sign:_____

Weekday:_____Moon Phase: _____ Moon Sign:_____

Occasion: _____Weather:_____

### Desire/Intentions

_____
_____
_____

### Ingredients/Materials

_____
_____
_____
_____
_____
_____
_____
_____

### Deities/Spirits          Offerings
### Elements Invoked

_____   _____
_____   _____
_____   _____
_____   _____
_____   _____
_____   _____
_____   _____

### Divination

_____
_____
_____
_____
_____
_____
_____
_____
_____
_____
_____

Altar Set Up

Ritual/Spell

# Ritual

Date: _____ Time: _____ Sun Sign:_____

Weekday:_____Moon Phase: _____ Moon Sign:_____

Occasion: _____Weather:_____

## Desire/Intentions

## Ingredients/Materials

## Deities/Spirits
Elements Invoked                    Offerings

## Divination

## Altar Set Up

## Ritual/Spell

# Ritual

Date: _____ Time: _____ Sun Sign:_____

Weekday:_____ Moon Phase: _____ Moon Sign:_____

Occasion: _____ Weather:_____

## Desire/Intentions

## Ingredients/Materials

## Deities/Spirits          Offerings
Elements Invoked

## Divination

Altar Set Up

Ritual/Spell

# Ritual

Date: _____ Time: _____ Sun Sign:_____

Weekday:_____Moon Phase: _____ Moon Sign:_____

Occasion: _____Weather:_____

Desire/Intentions

Ingredients/Materials

Deities/Spirits
Elements Invoked

Offerings

Divination

## Altar Set Up

## Ritual/Spell

# Ritual

Date: _____ Time: _____ Sun Sign:_____

Weekday:_____Moon Phase: _____ Moon Sign:_____

Occasion: _____Weather:_____

---

Desire/Intentions

_____

_____

_____

---

Ingredients/Materials

_____

_____

_____

_____

_____

_____

_____

_____

_____

---

Deities/Spirits          Offerings
Elements Invoked

_____        _____

_____        _____

_____        _____

_____        _____

_____        _____

_____        _____

---

Divination

_____

_____

_____

_____

_____

_____

_____

_____

Altar Set Up

Ritual/Spell

# Ritual

Date: _____ Time: _____ Sun Sign:_____

Weekday:_____ Moon Phase: _____ Moon Sign:_____

Occasion: _____ Weather:_____

## Desire/Intentions

_____

_____

_____

## Ingredients/Materials

_____

_____

_____

_____

_____

_____

_____

## Deities/Spirits Elements Invoked        Offerings

_____    _____

_____    _____

_____    _____

_____    _____

_____    _____

_____    _____

## Divination

_____

_____

_____

_____

_____

_____

_____

Altar Set Up

Ritual/Spell

# Ritual

Date: _____ Time: _____ Sun Sign:_____

Weekday:_____Moon Phase: _____ Moon Sign:_____

Occasion: _____Weather:_____

### Desire/Intentions

### Ingredients/Materials

### Deities/Spirits          Offerings
Elements Invoked

### Divination

Altar Set Up

Ritual/Spell

# Ritual

Date: _____ Time: _____ Sun Sign:_____

Weekday:_____ Moon Phase: _____ Moon Sign:_____

Occasion: _____ Weather:_____

## Desire/Intentions

_____
_____
_____
_____

## Ingredients/Materials

_____
_____
_____
_____
_____
_____
_____
_____
_____

## Deities/Spirits Elements Invoked    Offerings

_____     _____
_____     _____
_____     _____
_____     _____
_____     _____
_____     _____
_____     _____

## Divination

_____
_____
_____
_____
_____
_____
_____
_____
_____
_____

## Altar Set Up

## Ritual/Spell

# Ritual

Date: _____ Time: _____ Sun Sign:_____

Weekday:_____Moon Phase: _____ Moon Sign:_____

Occasion: _____ Weather:_____

## Desire/Intentions

## Ingredients/Materials

## Deities/Spirits
Elements Invoked

## Offerings

## Divination

Altar Set Up

Ritual/Spell

# Ritual

Date: _____ Time: _____ Sun Sign:_____
Weekday:_____ Moon Phase: _____ Moon Sign:_____
Occasion: _____ Weather:_____

Desire/Intentions

Ingredients/Materials

Deities/Spirits                    Offerings
Elements Invoked

Divination

## Altar Set Up

## Ritual/Spell

# DIVINATION

# Divination

*Divination: the act of seeking knowledge.*

How do you divine? The divination pages have been set up to accommodate any type of divination method. Whether you use tarot cards, lenormand decks, spirit or oracle cards, runes or pendants, you should be able to use this section to its full extent!

There are pages for smaller spreads like your daily pull and three card spreads, and larger sections that allow you to draw in the spread that you used.

If you want to create your own spreads, I suggest sitting down and thinking about what you want the deck to tell you. When I'm creating mine, I think about the who, what, where, when, why and how of what I want to know. From there I can usually pinpoint questions or phrases to use in the actual spread. Think of your questions first, because that will give you the amount of cards for the spread. If you choose the card count first, it might stress you out that you can't find enough, or too many questions, for your spread.

Eg:
What: Situational Clarity
Who: Me
When: Present/Near Future/Distant Future.
Where: My mind. My emotion. My body. My soul,
My family. My life.
Why: Am I stuck. Am I worried. Am I frustrated.
Am I blind.
How: Things that will help. Things that will hinder.

In the back of the journal you'll also find 3 pages of well known spreads, both small with 3 cards or less, and larger ones like The Celtic Cross and Year in Advance, as well as an easy break down of the basic tarot card meanings.

# Try it out!

In the space below, think of something you'd like to have the answer to, or a tarot spread for.

What:_____

Who: _____

When: _____

Where: _____

Why: _____

How: _____

Questions you came up with for your spread:

_____

_____

_____

_____

_____

_____

Draw out the cards below, however you want:

Date:___/___/___.

Question(s) Asked: _____
_____

Pulled/Picked: _____

Interpretation: _____
_____
_____
_____
_____
_____
_____
_____
_____

Date:___/___/___.

Question(s) Asked: _____
_____

Pulled/Picked: _____

Interpretation: _____
_____
_____
_____
_____
_____
_____
_____
_____

Date:___/___/___.

Question(s) Asked: _____
_____

Pulled/Picked: _____

Interpretation: _____
_____
_____
_____
_____
_____
_____
_____
_____

Date:___/___/___.

Question(s) Asked: _____
_____

Pulled/Picked: _____

Interpretation: _____
_____
_____
_____
_____
_____
_____
_____
_____

Date:___/___/___.

Question(s) Asked: _____

_____

Pulled/Picked: _____

Interpretation: _____

_____

_____

_____

_____

_____

_____

_____

_____

Date:___/___/___.

Question(s) Asked: _____

_____

Pulled/Picked: _____

Interpretation: _____

_____

_____

_____

_____

_____

_____

_____

_____

Date:___/___/___.

Question(s) Asked: _____

_____

Pulled/Picked: _____

Interpretation: _____

_____

_____

_____

_____

_____

_____

_____

_____

Date:___/___/___.

Question(s) Asked: _____

_____

Pulled/Picked: _____

Interpretation: _____

_____

_____

_____

_____

_____

_____

_____

_____

Date:____/____/____.

Question(s) Asked: _____
_____

Pulled/Picked: _____

Interpretation: _____
_____
_____
_____
_____
_____
_____
_____
_____

Date:____/____/____.

Question(s) Asked: _____
_____

Pulled/Picked: _____

Interpretation: _____
_____
_____
_____
_____
_____
_____
_____
_____

Date:____/____/____.

Question(s) Asked: _____
_____

Pulled/Picked: _____

Interpretation: _____
_____
_____
_____
_____
_____
_____
_____
_____

Date:____/____/____.

Question(s) Asked: _____
_____

Pulled/Picked: _____

Interpretation: _____
_____
_____
_____
_____
_____
_____
_____
_____

Date:____/____/____.

Question(s) Asked: _____
_____

Pulled/Picked: _____

Interpretation: _____
_____
_____
_____
_____
_____
_____
_____
_____

Date:____/____/____.

Question(s) Asked: _____
_____

Pulled/Picked: _____

Interpretation: _____
_____
_____
_____
_____
_____
_____
_____
_____

Date:____/____/____.

Question(s) Asked: _____
_____

Pulled/Picked: _____

Interpretation: _____
_____
_____
_____
_____
_____
_____
_____
_____

Date:____/____/____.

Question(s) Asked: _____
_____

Pulled/Picked: _____

Interpretation: _____
_____
_____
_____
_____
_____
_____
_____
_____

Date:___/___/___.

Question(s) Asked: _____
_____
_____

Pulled/Picked: _____
_____

Interpretation: _____
_____
_____
_____
_____
_____
_____
_____
_____
_____

Date:___/___/___.

Question(s) Asked: _____
_____
_____

Pulled/Picked: _____
_____

Interpretation: _____
_____
_____
_____
_____
_____
_____
_____
_____
_____

Date:___/___/___.

Question(s) Asked: _____
_____
_____

Pulled/Picked: _____
_____

Interpretation: _____
_____
_____
_____
_____
_____
_____
_____
_____
_____

Date:___/___/___.

Question(s) Asked: _____
_____
_____

Pulled/Picked: _____
_____

Interpretation: _____
_____
_____
_____
_____
_____
_____
_____
_____
_____

Date:___/___/___.

Question(s) Asked: _____

Pulled/Picked: _____

Interpretation: _____

Date:___/___/___.

Question(s) Asked: _____

Pulled/Picked: _____

Interpretation: _____

Date:___/___/___.

Question(s) Asked: _____

Pulled/Picked: _____

Interpretation: _____

Date:___/___/___.

Question(s) Asked: _____

Pulled/Picked: _____

Interpretation: _____

Date:___/___/___.

Question(s) Asked: _____
_____
Pulled/Picked: _____
_____
Interpretation: _____
_____
_____
_____
_____
_____
_____
_____
_____

Date:___/___/___.

Question(s) Asked: _____
_____
Pulled/Picked: _____
_____
Interpretation: _____
_____
_____
_____
_____
_____
_____
_____
_____

Date:___/___/___.

Question(s) Asked: _____
_____
Pulled/Picked: _____
_____
Interpretation: _____
_____
_____
_____
_____
_____
_____
_____
_____

Date:___/___/___.

Question(s) Asked: _____
_____
Pulled/Picked: _____
_____
Interpretation: _____
_____
_____
_____
_____
_____
_____
_____
_____

Date:___/___/___.

Question(s) Asked: _____
_____

Pulled/Picked: _____

Interpretation: _____
_____
_____
_____
_____
_____
_____
_____
_____

Date:___/___/___.

Question(s) Asked: _____
_____

Pulled/Picked: _____

Interpretation: _____
_____
_____
_____
_____
_____
_____
_____
_____

Date:___/___/___.

Question(s) Asked: _____
_____

Pulled/Picked: _____

Interpretation: _____
_____
_____
_____
_____
_____
_____
_____
_____

Date:___/___/___.

Question(s) Asked: _____
_____

Pulled/Picked: _____

Interpretation: _____
_____
_____
_____
_____
_____
_____
_____
_____

Date:___/___/___.

Question(s) Asked: _____
_____
_____

Pulled/Picked: _____
_____

Interpretation: _____
_____
_____
_____
_____
_____
_____
_____
_____
_____

Date:___/___/___.

Question(s) Asked: _____
_____
_____

Pulled/Picked: _____
_____

Interpretation: _____
_____
_____
_____
_____
_____
_____
_____
_____
_____

Date:___/___/___.

Question(s) Asked: _____
_____
_____

Pulled/Picked: _____
_____

Interpretation: _____
_____
_____
_____
_____
_____
_____
_____
_____
_____

Date:___/___/___.

Question(s) Asked: _____
_____
_____

Pulled/Picked: _____
_____

Interpretation: _____
_____
_____
_____
_____
_____
_____
_____
_____
_____

Date:___/___/___.

Question(s) Asked: _____

_____

Pulled/Picked: _____

Interpretation: _____

Date:___/___/___.

Question(s) Asked: _____

_____

Pulled/Picked: _____

Interpretation: _____

Date:___/___/___.

Question(s) Asked: _____

_____

Pulled/Picked: _____

Interpretation: _____

Date:___/___/___.

Question(s) Asked: _____

_____

Pulled/Picked: _____

Interpretation: _____

Date:____/____/____.

Spread:_____

Card(s):_____

_____

_____

Interpretation:_____

_____

_____

_____

_____

_____

_____

_____

_____

_____

_____

_____

_____

Date:____/____/____.

Spread:
Card(s):

Interpretation:

Date: ___/___/___.

Spread: _____

Card(s): _____
_____
_____
_____

Interpretation: _____
_____
_____
_____
_____
_____
_____
_____
_____
_____
_____
_____
_____
_____

Date:____/____/____.

Spread:
Card(s):

Interpretation:

Date:___/___/___.

Spread:_____
Card(s):_____
_____
_____
_____

Interpretation:_____
_____
_____
_____
_____
_____
_____
_____
_____
_____
_____
_____

Date:___/___/___.

Spread:
Card(s):

Interpretation:

Date:_____/_____/_____.

Spread:_____

Card(s):_____

_____

_____

_____

Interpretation:_____

_____

_____

_____

_____

_____

_____

_____

_____

_____

_____

_____

_____

Date:___/___/___.

Spread:
Card(s):

Interpretation:

Date:___/___/___.

Spread:_____
Card(s):_____
_____
_____
_____

Interpretation:_____
_____
_____
_____
_____
_____
_____
_____
_____
_____
_____
_____
_____
_____

Date:___/___/___.

Spread:
Card(s):

Interpretation:

Date:____/____/____.



Spread:_____
Card(s):_____
_____
_____
_____
_____

Interpretation:_____
_____
_____
_____
_____
_____
_____
_____
_____
_____
_____
_____

Date:____/____/____.

Spread:
Card(s):

Interpretation:

# INVENTORY

# Inventory

All Out Of...

All Out Of...

# Inventory

All Out Of...

All Out Of...

# Inventory

All Out Of...

All Out Of...

# Inventory

## All Out Of...

## All Out Of...

# Grimoire

# Colours
## Candles, clothes, sachets

| | |
|---|---|
| Black | Divination, protection, banishing |
| White | Cleansing, healing, protection (can be used in place of any other candle colour) |
| Gray | Vision, absorbs negativity |
| Brown | Stability, integrity, concentration, grounding |
| Blue | Truth, tranquility, psychic ability |
| Green | Growth, healing, abundance, money, luck |
| Orange | Courage, pride, ambition, success |
| Red | Sexual love, lust, passion, strength, |
| Pink | Compassion, harmony, love, affection, friendship |
| Purple | Psychic ability, insight, self-esteem |
| Yellow | Joy, intelligence, creativity, happiness |
| Gold | Vitality, strength, success, mal archetype |
| Silver | Intuition, balance, receptivity, female archetype |

# Crystals
## Alphabetical by use

Here you'll find a list of crystals for the most commonly asked about intentions and issues. I've tried to include as many crystal options as possible, while sticking to the ones most likely found in occult shops or online that won't cost you an arm and a leg.

*Keep in mind a few things when buying crystals: choose intuitively, even if it doesn't match up with the below tables, they like to be separated from other crystals when not in use, they also like wood boxes, and try to figure out how ethically sourced they are before buying.*

| | |
|---|---|
| Abundance | Aventurine, Bloodstone, Chrysoprase, Citrine, Green Tourmaline, Jade, Malachite, Moss Agate, Peridot, Rhodochrosite, Smokey Quartz, Quartz, Salt, Tigers Eye, Topaz, Tree Agate, Watermelon Tourmaline |
| Awaken, Activate (potential, power) | Aventurine, Chrysoprase, Clear Quartz, Fluorite, Hematite, Iolite, Kunzite, Rhodochrosite, Rhodonite, Rose Quartz |
| Anxiety (ease/release) | Agate, Amazonite, Chrysocolla, Chrysoprase, Green Aventurine, Hematite, Howlite, Kyanite |
| Balance | Amazonite, Amber, Amethyst, Apache Tears, Aragonite, Aventurine, Brown Jasper, Chrysocolla, Citrine, Clear Quartz, Fluorite, Garnet, Green Jasper, Green Tourmaline, Hawk's Eye, Hematite, Lepidolite, Obsidian, Onyx, Peridot, Rhodochrosite, Rhodonite, Serpentine, Smokey Quartz, Sodalite, Tigers Eye, Tree Agate, Turquoise, Watermelon Tourmaline |
| Banish | Aquamarine, Aventurine, Beryl, Bloodstone, Chrysoprase, Red Jasper, Rhodonite, Salt |
| Calm (most light blue stones) | Agate, Amazonite, Amber, Amethyst, Aragonite, Chrysocolla, Clear Quartz, Garnet, Fluorite, Hematite, Iolite, Jet, Kunzite, Lepidolite, Malachite, Moonstone, Morganite, Moss Agate, Peridot, Pink Calcite, Pink Sapphire, Pink Tourmaline,, Rose Quartz, Selenite, Tigers Eye |
| Clarity | Amazonite, Amber, Ametrine, Apache Tears, Apophyllite, Aquamarine, Aventurine, Blue Lace Agate, Blue Topaz, Blue Tourmaline, Clear Calcite, Clear Quartz, Celestite, Citrine, Danburite,, Hawk's Eye, Hematite, Jade, Kyanite, Labradorite, Obsidian, Rhodonite, Selenite, Tiger's Eye, Turquoise, White Diamond |

# Crystals
## Alphabetical by use

| | |
|---|---|
| Communication | Amazonite, Amethyst, Angelite, Apatite, Aquamarine, Azurite, Black Agate, Blue Lace Agate, Blue Topaz, Clear Calcite, Clear Quartz, Chrysocolla, Chrysoprase, Danburite, Fluorite, Iolite, Jasper, Kunzite, Kyanite, Lapis Lazuli, Lodestone, Malachite, Moonstone, Morganite, Moss Agate, Sapphire, Selenite, Sodalite, Tanzanite, Tigers Eye, Turquoise. |
| Courage | Amazonite, Amber, Aquamarine, Aventurine, Black Agate, Bloodstone, Brown Agate, Brown Tourmaline, Carnelian, Chrysoprase, Danburite, Diamond, Hematite, Herkimer Diamond, Hessonite Garnet, Jade, Jasper, Labradorite, Lapis Lazuli, Orange Calcite, Red Agate, Red Banded Agate, Sapphire, Sardonyx, Snakeskin Agate, Tigers Eye, Topaz, Turquoise |
| Creativity | Agate, Amber, Amethyst, Apatite, Aquamarine, Blue Topaz, Blue Tourmaline, Carnelian, Cat's Eye, Chrysocolla, Citrine, Emerald, Fluorite, Green Aventurine, green Tourmaline, Howlite, Kyanite, Lapis Lazuli, Moonstone, Moss Agate, Orange Calcite, Obsidian, Opal, Red Garnet, Red Tourmaline, Ruby, Rutilated Quartz, Smokey Quartz, Tiger's Eye, Turquoise, Watermelon Tourmaline, White Quartz |
| Decision | Ametrine, Aventurine, Azurite, Bloodstone, Carnelian, Jade, Onyx, Selenite |
| Divination | Amethyst, Azurite, Clear Quartz, Fluorite, Hematite, Jet, Lapis Lazuli, Malachite, Moonstone, Obsidian, Pyrite, Red Jasper, Tiger's Eye, Topaz |
| Fear (dealing with) | Amazonite, Amber, Amethyst, Apache Tears, Aquamarine, Azurite, Beryl, Black Tourmaline, Bloodstone, Carnelian, Charoite, Chrysocolla, Citrine, Jasper, Jet, Obsidian, Onyx, Opal, Peridot, Red Banded Agate, Rutilated Quartz, Smokey Quartz, Sodalite, Sunstone, Tiger's Eye, Topaz |
| Forgiveness | Angelite, Apache Tears, Blue Topaz, Chrysoprase, Lodestone, Rhodochrosite, Rhodonite |
| Friendship | Agate, Aventurine, Blue Lace Agate, Clear Quartz, Emerald, Garnet, Lapis Lazuli, Lodestone, Moonstone, Rhodochrosite, Rose Quartz, Sapphire, Sard, Smithsonite, Turquoise |

# Crystals
## Alphabetical by use

| | |
|---|---|
| Grounding | Agate, Amazonite, Amethyst, Andalusite, Apache Tears, Aragonite, Black Garnet, Black Tourmaline, Brown Jade, Brown Jasper, Brown Zircon, Blue Lace Agate, Chrysocolla, Fluorite, Green Jasper, Hematite, Jet, Kunzite, Lodestone, Malachite, Obsidian, Onyx, Peridot, Petrified Wood, Pink Calcite, Red Jasper, Salt, Smokey Quartz, Sugilite, Tiger's Eye, Turquoise, Unakite |
| Happiness | Amber, Apophyllite, Aquamarine, Aventurine, Blue Lace Agate, Blue Quartz, Black Tourmaline, Brown Agate, Cat's Eye, Chrysoprase, Green Zircon, Hematite, Moonstone, Moss Agate, Peridot, Rhodonite, Rose Quartz, Ruby, Spessartite Garnet, Turquoise, Yellow Zircon |
| Healing | Agates, Amber, Amethyst, Ametrine, Apatite, Aquamarine, Aventurine, Azurite, Bloodstone, Blue Lace Agate, Calcite, Carnelian, Celestite, Chrysoprase, Citrine, Emerald, Garnet, Hematite, Jaspers, Jet, Kunzite, Lavender Jade, Lodestone, Malachite, Moonstone, Peridot, Ruby, Salt, Sugilite, Sunstone, Tiger's Eye, Topaz, Tourmalines, Turquoise. |
| Heartbreak (recovering) | Aventurine, Blue Calcite, Blue Topaz, Chrysocolla, Chrysoprase, Garnet, Jade, Lapis Lazuli, Morganite, Rose Quartz |
| Inspiration | Amazonite, Amethyst, Ametrine, Apatite, Aquamarine, Blue Lace Agate, Blue Topaz, Carnelian, Clear Quartz, Celestite, Charoite, Chrysocolla, Green Tourmaline, Jade, Labradorite, Onyx, Opal, Peridot, Rhodolite Garnet, Selenite, Serpentine, Tiger's Eye, Turquoise |
| Intuition | Alexandrite, Amazonite, Amethyst, Ametrine, Apophyllite, Azurite, Blue Topaz, Blue Tourmaline, Fluorite, Green Calcite, Hematite, Iolite, Labradorite, Lapis Lazuli, Lodestone, Moonstone, Orange Calcite, Rhodolite Garnet, Rhodonite, Sodalite, Turquoise |
| Kindness | Chrysoprase, Jade, Rhodochrosite |
| Loss (dealing with) | Ametrine, Charoite, Hematite, Kyanite, Moldovite, Phenacite, Tiger's Eye, Topaz. |
| Love | Alexandrite, Amazonite, Amethyst(*manifest*), Aventurine, Bloodstone, Desert Rose, Emerald(*secure*), Green Agate, Lepidolite, Lodestone, Malachite, Pink Calcite, Pink Jasper, Pink Sapphire, Red Agate, Red Tourmaline, Rhodochrosite(*new*), Rhodolite Garnet, Sard, Sugilite, Tanzanite, Turquoise, Zoisite. |

# Crystals
## Alphabetical by use

| | |
|---|---|
| **Luck**<br>most green stones | Amber, Apache Tears, Brown Jasper, Black Tourmaline, Cat's Eye, Chrysoprase, Citrine, Emerald, Fluorite, Garnet, Green Aventurine, Green Jasper, Jet, Lepidolite, Malachite, Moonstone, Obsidian, Opal, Pyrite, Reddish Brown Aventurine, Red Jasper, Sardonyx, Smokey Quartz, Staurolite, Tiger's Eye, Topaz, Turquoise. |
| **Money**<br>most green sones | Amazonite, Brown Agate, Brown Zircon, Bloodstone, Chrysoprase, Emerald, Green Aventurine, Green Calcite, Green Jasper, Green Tourmaline, Green Zircon, Herkimer Diamond, Jade Lodestone, Malachite, Moss Agate, Peridot, Pyrite, Red Spinel, Red Zircon, Staurolite, Topaz. |
| **Negativity**<br>(banish & release) | Amazonite, Amethyst, Ametrine, Andalusite, Apache Tears, Apatite, Aventurine, Black Tourmaline, Carnelian, Charoite, Citrine, Clear Quartz, Garnet, Hawk's Eye, Hematite, Jade, Jet, Larimar, Lepidolite, Lodestone, Malachite, Onyx, Peridot, Red Jasper, Rose Quartz, Sea Salt, Selenite, Smokey Quartz, Snowflake Obsidian, Sugilite, Turquoise, Unakite |
| **Overcome Obstacles** | Azurite, Bloodstone, Black Tourmaline, Blue Lace Agate, Carnelian, Kunzite, Moonstone, Obsidian, Opal, Peridot, Petrified Wood, Pink Tourmaline, Smokey Quartz, Sugilite |
| **Patience** | Amber, Azurite, Blue Jade, Blue Lace Agate, Chrysoprase, Danburite, Garnet, Howlite, Morganite, Onyx, Rhodonite. |
| **Peace** | Amber, Apache Tears, Black Agate, Blue Diamond, Blue Topaz, Brown Tourmaline, Carnelian, Herkimer Diamond, Jade, Jasper, Kunzite, Lepidolite, Malachite, Obsidian, Peridot, Red Agate, Red Zircon, Ruby, Sapphire, Selenite, Sodalite, Sugilite, Turquoise, Yellow Zircon |
| **Protection** | *Emotional:* Obsidian, Ruby. *Psychic:* Angelite, Calcite, Carnelian, Salt, Tiger's Eye. *Spiritual:* Angelite, Calcite, Tiger's Eye. *Travel:* Lapis Lazuli, Moonstone. *General:* Amber, Amethyst, Apache Tears, Aquamarine, Aventurine, Banded Agate, Black Agate, Black Tourmaline, Cat's Eye, Chrysoprase, Clear Quartz, Emerald, Garnet, Hematite, Jade, Jet, Kunzite, Lepidolite, Lodestone, Malachite, Onyx, Orange Calcite, Peridot, Petrified Wood, Pyrite, Red Agate, Red Jasper, Rose Quartz, Ruby, Sard, Sardonyx, Serpentine, Snowflake Obsidian, Sunstone, Topaz, Turquoise, Watermelon Tourmaline, Yellow Quartz, Zircon |

# Crystals
## Alphabetical by use

| | |
|---|---|
| Psychic Ability | Amethyst, Angelite, Apache Tears, Apatite, Aquamarine, Azurite, Beryl, Blue Calcite, Blue Topaz, Citrine, Clear Quartz, Danburite, Emerald, Hawk's Eye, Iolite, Jet, Lapis Lazuli, Lepidolite, Malachite, Moonstone, Smokey Quartz, Tiger's Eye, Tourmaline. |
| Purification | Amber, Amethyst, Ametrine, Aquamarine, Azurite, Aragonite, Black Tourmaline, Blue Calcite, Blue Topaz, Charoite, Clear Quartz, Green Fluorite, Garnet, Gold, Jade, Lodestone, Peridot, Salt, Silver, Smokey Quartz, Tiger's Eye, Turquoise |
| Sleep | Amber, Amethyst, Blue Topaz, Blue Tourmaline, Citrine, Green Jasper, Jet, Lodestone, Malachite, Moonstone, Peridot |
| Strength | Amazonite, Amber, Amethyst, Angelite, Aquamarine, Azurite, Bloodstone, Clear Quartz, Dioptase, Green Tourmaline, Fluorite, Hematite, Iolite, Lapis Lazui, Malachite, Moss Agate, Opal, Peridot, Red Garnet, Red Jasper, Red Tourmaline, Red Zicon, Rhodochrosite, Ruby, Snakeskin Agate Sunstone. |
| Stress (relief) | Amber, Ametrine, Apophyllite, Aquamarine, Aragonite, Azurite, Bloodstone, Blue Lace Agate, Blue Jade, Blue Quartz, Blue Tourmaline, Carnelian, Celestite, Chrysocolla, Chrysoprase, Hematite, Howlite, Jasper, Kunzite, Labradorite, Lepidolite, Moonstone, Onyx, Peridot, Pink Tourmaline, Rose Quartz, Sodalite, Sugilite, Tiger's Eye, Topaz, Turquoise |
| Transfor-mation | Alexandrite, Amber, Amethyst, Azurite, Blue Lace Agate, Charoite, Green Apophyllite, Jet, Labradorite, Malachite, Moldovite, Obsidian, Onyx, Quartz, Smokey Quartz, Sodalite, Staurolite, Tourmaline, Unakite. |
| Willpower | Chrysoprase, Citrine, Fluorite, Green Tourmaline, Hematite, Lodestone, Onyx, Pyrite, Rhodochrosite, Rutilated Quartz, Tanzanite, Tiger's Eye, Yellow Jasper |
| Wisdom | Amber, Amethyst, Apache Tears, Apophyllite, Aquamarine, Azurite, Blue Lace Agate, Carnelian, Celestite, Charoite, Chrysocollla, Chrysoprase, Desert Rose, Dioptase, Garnet, Howlite, Jade, Jasoerm Labradorite, Lapis Lazuli, Moonstone, Opal, Peridot, Quartz, Red Spinel, Red Tourmaline, Red Zircon, Rhodonite, Sardonyx, Smokey Quartz, Snowflake Obsidian, Sodalite, Sugilite, Tanzanite, Tiger's Eye, Tree Agate(*Dendritic*), Topaz |

# Crystals

| | |
|---|---|
| | |
| | |
| | |
| | |
| | |
| | |
| | |
| | |

# Days of the Week

| Day | Intentions | Correspondences |
|-----|------------|-----------------|
| **Monday** | Clairvoyance, Creativity, Dreamwork, Fertility, Healing, The Home, Inspiration, Intuition, Love, Protection, Psychic Ability, Travel, Truth | The Moon (planet), Pale Blue, Gray, Silver, White, Moonwort, Wormwood, Chamomile, Jasmine, Poppy, White Rose, Violet, Emerald, Moonstone, Clear Quartz, White Quartz |
| **Tuesday** | Action, Aggression, Assertiveness, Challenges, Courage, Discipline, Energy, Healing, Justice, Passion, Purification, Strength, Truth, War | Mars, Black, Orange, Red, Scarlet, Basil, Garlic, Snapdragon, Allspice, Ginger, Patchouli, Bloodstone, Emerald, Garnet, Ruby, Sapphire, Topaz |
| **Wednesday** | Business, Cleverness, Communication, Creativity, Crossroads, Divination, Fear, Insight, Introspection, Knowledge, Loss, Money, Self Improvement, Skills, Travel, Wisdom | Mercury, Orange, Purple, Violet, Silver, Yellow, Dill, Jasmine, Lavender, Lily of the Valley, Fern, Agate, Amethyst, Aventurine, Lodestone, Opal, Ruby, Turquoise |
| **Thursday** | Abundance, Business, Desire, Endurance, Fidelity, Honour, Justice, Leadership, Loyalty, Luck, Money, Prosperity, Relationships, Success, | Jupiter, Royal Blue, Green, Indigo, Purple, Honeysuckle, Sage, Cinnamon, Cinquefoil, Nutmeg, Wheat, Amethyst, Carnelian, Cat's Eye, Sapphire, Turquoise |
| **Friday** | Beauty, Emotions, Fertility, Friendship, Happiness, Love, Magic, Passion, Pleasure, Romance, Sexuality, Wisdom | Venus, Aqua, Blue, Green, Indigo, Pink, Saffron, Sandalwood, Raspberry, Rose, Strawberry, Thyme, Violet, Alexandrite, Amber, Cat's Eye, Emerald, Rose Quartz, |
| **Saturday** | Banish, Bind, Boundaries, Business, Death, Freedom, Justice, Trauma, Life, Limitations, Money, Motivation, Negativity, Obstacles, Peace, Protection, Willpower, Wisdom | Saturn, Black, Grey, Indigo, Purple, Temperance, 2 of Swords, Knight of Swords, Morning Glory, Thyme, Mullein, Myrrh, Amethyst, Apache Tears, Diamond, Hematite, Jet, Labradorite, Turquoise |
| **Sunday** | Accomplishment, Action, Ambition, Beauty, Confidence, Creativity, Freedom, Friendship, Goals, Healing, Hope, Illumination, Justice, Leadership, Light, Money, Personal Growth, Personal Power, Pride, Prosperity, Protection, Spirituality, Strength, Success, Visions, Well-Being | The Sun, Gold, Gray, Orange, Pink, White, Yellow, Cinnamon, Frankincense, Carnation, Marigold, St. Johns Wort, Sunflower, Amber, Carnelian, Diamond, Clear Quartz, Sunstone, Tiger's Eye, Top |

# Divination Spreads

## 3-card spread

past / present / future
body / mind / soul
yesterday / today / tomorrow
me before / me now / future me

## 9-card spread

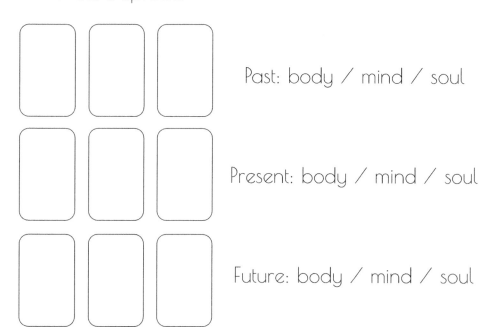

Past: body / mind / soul

Present: body / mind / soul

Future: body / mind / soul

## clarity spread

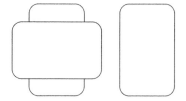

situation & opposing factor
solution

# Divination Spreads

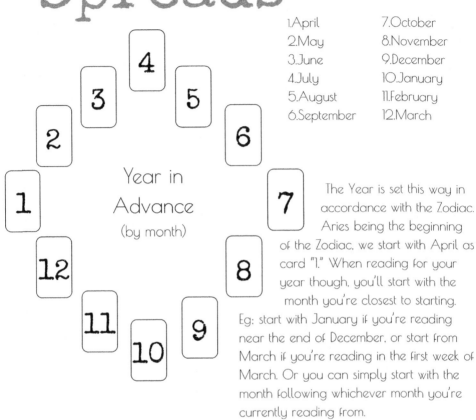

1. April
2. May
3. June
4. July
5. August
6. September

7. October
8. November
9. December
10. January
11. February
12. March

## Year in Advance
### (by month)

The Year is set this way in accordance with the Zodiac. Aries being the beginning of the Zodiac, we start with April as card "1." When reading for your year though, you'll start with the month you're closest to starting. Eg: start with January if you're reading near the end of December, or start from March if you're reading in the first week of March. Or you can simply start with the month following whichever month you're currently reading from.

## week in advance

M T W T F S S

## month in advance
### (by week)

## year in advance
### (by quarter)

1 2 3 4

1. Jan-Mar
3. July-Sept

2. Apr-June
4. Oct-Dec

# Divination Spreads

## Celtic Cross

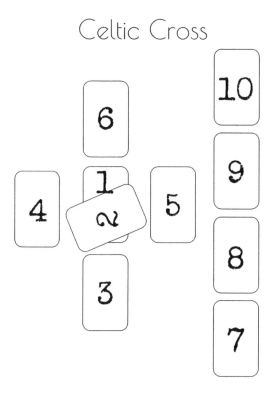

1. Heart of the matter

2. Opposing factor

3. Root cause

4. Past

5. Future

6. Goal

7. You now

8. External influence

9. Hopes and fears

10. Outcome

# Herbs
## Alphabetical by use

       Here is your list of herbs, for the same uses as in the crystal section of this journal. What should be remembered is that not everything here is an herb, it can be a plant or a flower, and most importantly **SHOULD NOT BE INGESTED UNLESS SAFE TO DO SO.**

       If you're looking to make something that can be drank, please find herbs that can be found already in tea bags, as they have been processed properly and portioned safely in order to be consumed. If you can't find it in a tea, a good rule is don't ingest.

       Stick to putting your materials inside of glass bottles or cloth sachets for your spells, or simply putting together a bouquet of flowers that promotes your intent. (Eg: happiness, peace, love, etc.)

| | |
|---|---|
| Abundance | Bluebell, Grape, Honeysuckle |
| Awaken, Activate (potential, power) | Ginseng, Lemon Balm, Mistletoe, Patchouli, Peppermint, Sandalwood, Thyme |
| Anxiety (ease/release) | Bergamot, Chamomile, Frankincense, Garlic, Germanium, Jasmine, Lavender, Lemon Balm, Monkshood, Passionflower, Pennyroyal Peony, Primrose, Valerian, Vervain, Wormwood |
| Balance | Angelica, Basil, Bergamot, Bluebell, Carnation, Chamomile, Comfrey, Geranium, Honeysuckle, Ivy, Lilac, Primrose, Sage, Sunflower, Sweet Woodruff, Vervain, Yarrow |
| Banish | Agrimony, Angelica, Basil, Black Cohosh, Broom, Clover, Comfrey, Fern, Frankincense, Garlic, Heliotrope, Lilac, Meadowsweet, Mugwort, Mullein, Patchouli, Peony, Peppermint, Rose, Rosemary, Rue, Sandalwood, St. John's Wort, Snapdragon, Solomon's Seal, Vervain, Violet, Yarrow |
| Calm | Anemone, Angelica, Aster, Bergamot, Belladonna, Borage, Broom, Cardamom, Carnation, Clover, Daffodil, Daisy, Dill, Ginger, Ginseng, Heliotrope, Henbane, Holy Basil, Honeysuckle, Jasmine, Lemon Balm, Lily of the Valley, Marjoram, Monkshood, Passionflower, Rose, Saffron, Sandalwood, Sweet Woodruff, Thyme, Valerian, Vanilla, Yarrow |
| Clarity | Basil, Dandelion, Frankincense, Grape, Heather, Honeysuckle, Iris, Jasmine, Lavender, Lemon Balm, Passionflower, Peppermint, Periwinkle, Raspberry, Rue, Sandalwood, Sunflower, White Rose |
| Communication | Allspice, Blackberry/Bramble, Broom, Chamomile, Daisy, Dandelion, Fennel, Garlic, Geranium, Jasmine, Lavender, Lily, Marigold, Nettle, Orris Root, Rosemary, Valerian, White Violet, Yellow Carnation |

# Herbs
## Alphabetical by use

| | |
|---|---|
| Courage | Allspice, Basil, Bergamot, Borage, Cardamom, Catnip, Clove, Columbine, Fennel, Frankincense, Galangal, Garlic, Geranium, Ginger, Heliotrope, Lady's Mantle, Lavender, Mandrake, Mullein, Nettle, Pepper, Rose, Rosemary, St. John's Wort, Thistle, Thyme, Witch Hazel, Wormwood, Yarrow |
| Creativity | Broom, Carnation, Cardamom, Chamomile, Cinnamon, Daisy, Honeysuckle, Iris, Lavender, Lilac, lily, Patchouli, Peppermint, Rose, Rosemary, Sandalwood, Valerian, Vervain, Yellow Jasmine |
| Decision | Apple, Solomon's Seal |
| Divination | Angelica, Basil, Broom, Daisy, Dandelion, Gorse, Hibiscus, Honeysuckle, Ivy, Lavender, Lilac, Marigold, Morning Glory, Mugwort, Peppermint, Rose, Rue, Sage, St. John's Wort, Strawberry, Sweet Woodruff, Thyme Vervain, Yarrow |
| Fear (dealing with) | Allspice, Bluebell, Cinnamon, Clover, Daffodil, Frankincense, Garlic, Geranium, Monkshood, Morning Flory, Nettle, Pepper, Primrose, Raspberry, Sage, Skullcap, St. John's Wort, Thistle, Yarrow |
| Forgiveness | Geranium, Rowan, Wormwood |
| Friendship | Allspice, Aloe, Angelica, Basil, Bluebell, Catnip, Clove, Cover, Daffodil, Gardenia, Geranium, Honeysuckle, Ivy, Laender, Lilac, Passionflower, Periwinkle, Pink Rose, Primrose, Rosemary, Strawberry, Sweet Woodruff, White Jasmine, Yarrow |
| Grounding | Blackberry/Bramble, Chamomile, Lavender, Myrrh, Patchouli, Red Clover, Rowan, Sage, Sandalwood, Vervain, Water Lily |
| Happiness | Aster, Basil, Bergamot, Blackberry/Bramble, Borage, Catnip, Clove, Coriander, Frankincense, Gardenia, Geranium, Heliotrope, Honeysuckle, Hyacinth, Jasmine, Lilac, Lily of the Valley, Marigold, Marjoram, Meadowsweet, Morning Glory, Mugwort, Mushroom, Rose, St. John's Wort, Patchouli, Saffron, Sunflower, Thyme, Valerian, Vanilla, Violet, Water Lily, Yarrow |
| Healing | Allspice, Aloe, Amaranth, Basil, Betony, Blessed Thistle, Blackberry/Bramble, Broom, Burdock, Cardamom, Carnation, Chamomile, Cinnamon, Clove, Clover, Comfrey, Coriander, Daisy, Dandelion, Fennel, Feverfew, Foxglove, Frankincense, Garlic, Gardenia, Geranium, Ginger, Heather, Heliotrope, Honeysuckle, Horehound, Ivy, Jasmine, Lavender, Lemon Balm, Lily of the Valley, Mandrake, Marigold, Marjoram, Mistletoe, Mugwort, Myrrh, Nettle, Pennyroyal, Peppermint, Rose, Rosemary, Rue, Saffron, Sage, Sandalwood, St. John's Wort, Spearmint, Sweet Woodruff, Thistle, Thyme, Valerian, Vervain, Violet, Wormwood, Yarrow |

# Herbs
## Alphabetical by use

| | |
|---|---|
| Heartbreak (recovering) | Amaranth, Cinnamon, Coriander, Feverfew, Gardenia, Lavender, Lemon Balm, Myrrh, Rosemary, White Rose |
| Inspiration | Angelica, Cinnamon, Clove, Frankincense, Grape, Ginger, Honeysuckle, Iris, Jasmine, Lavender, Lilac, Lily of the Valley, Lotus, Reed, Rose, Rosemary, Rue, Sandalwood, Vanilla, Vervain |
| Intuition | Blackberry/Bramble, Broom, Chamomile, Clover, Eyebright, Honeysuckle, Lavender, Rosemary, Solomon's Seal |
| Kindness | Allspice, Bluebell, Clover, Flax, Hyacinth |
| Loss (dealing with) | Anise, Comfrey, Fennel, Goldenrod, Jasmine, Morning Glory, Pomegranate, White Rose, Witch Hazel |
| Love | Basil, Carnation, Red Chrysanthemum, Daffodil, Daisy, Dill, Fern, Feverfew, Heather, Heliotrope, Honeysuckle, Iris, Ivy, Lilac, Lily of the Valley, Marigold, Marjoram, Mugwort, Pennyroyal, Periwinkle, Popp, Rose, Rue, Sage, Spearmint, Thyme, Valerian, Violet, Yarrow |
| Luck | Blackberry/Bramble, Bluebell, Chamomile, Daffodil, Daisy, Dill, Fern, Four-Leaf Clover, Galangal, Ginger, Heather, Iris, Irish Moss, Ivy, Jasmine, Lady's Mantle, Lavender, Lilac, Mistletoe, Nettle, Patchouli, Peony, Peppermint, Red Clover, Rose, Rosemary, Rue, Sandalwood St. Johns Wort, Spearmint, Sunflower, Violet, Thyme, Yarrow |
| Money | Anise, Basil, Bergamot, Blackberry/Bramble, Blue Iris, Borage, Chamomile, Cinnamon, Clover, Comfrey, Dandelion, Dill, Fennel, Fern, Flax, Galangal, Gardenia, Grape, Heliotrope, Honeysuckle, Lemon Balm, Mandrake, Marjoram, Mustard, Nutmeg, Patchouli, Peppermint, Periwinkle, Poppy, Saffron, Sage, St. John's Wort, Snapdragon, Spearmint, Sunflower, Sweet Woodruff, Thyme, Valerian, Vervain |
| Negativity (banish & release) | Angelia, Basil, Bluebell, Cinnamon, Clove, Columbine, Frankincense, Galangal, Ginseng, Ivy, Lavender, Lily, Lovage Mistletoe, Myrrh, Nettle, Patchouli, Pennyroyal, Peppermint, Rosemary, Rue, Sage, Sandalwood, Thyme, Violet, Yarrow |
| Overcome Obstacles | Bluebell, Broom, Dragon's Blood, Hibiscus, Mistletoe, Myrrh, Orris Root, Sage, Sunflower, Wormwood |
| Patience | Chamomile, Hawthorne, Iris, Rose, |
| Peace | Aloe, Angelica, Basil, Bergamot, Blue Violet, Catnip, Cinnamon, Coriander, Gardenia, Heather, Hibiscus, Honeysuckle, Jasmine, Lia, Lily of the Valley, Marigold, Meadowsweet, Mugwort, Morning Glory, Passionflower, Pennyroyal, Sage, St. John's Wort, Sunflower, Valerian, Vanilla, Vervain, White Lily |

# Herbs
## Alphabetical by use

| Protection | Agrimony, Aloe, Amaranth, Angelica, Bamboo Basil, Blackberry/ Bramble, Black Cohosh, Blessed Thistle, Broom, Carnation, Chrysanthemum, Cinnamon, Clove, Clover, Comfrey, Coriander, Dandelion, Dill, Fennel, Fern, Fir, Ginseng, Gorse, Hawthorn, Heather, Honeysuckle, Horehound, Ivy, Jasmine, Lavender, Lilac, Lily, Lily of the Valley, Mandrake, Marjoram, Mustard, Orris Root, Pennyroyal, Peony, Pepper, Periwinkle, Primrose, Raspberry, Rue, Sandalwood, Snapdragon, Solomon's Seal, Sweet Woodruff, Thistle, Thyme, Valerian, Vervain, Violet, Wormwood, Yarrow. |
|---|---|
| Psychic Ability | Anise, Basil, Borage, Catnip, Cinnamon, Clove, Comfrey, Dandelion, Eyebright, Flax, Frankincense, Galangal, Heather, Heliotrope, Hibiscus, Honeysuckle, Iris, Jasmine, Lavender, Marigold, Mugwort, Mullein, Myrrh, Nutmeg, Peppermint, Rose, Rosemary, Saffron, Sage, Sandalwood, Thyme, Wormwood, Yarrow |
| Purification | Aloe, Angelica, Basil, Broom, Burdock, Chamomile, Cinnamon, Clove, Dill, Fennel, Fern, Feverfew, Frankincense, Garlic, Geranium, Heather, Hyacinth, Iris, Jasmine, Lavender, Lila, Lovage, Marjoram, Mistletoe, Mugwort, Mustard, Myrrh, Nettle, Passionflower, Patchouli, Pennyroyal, Peppermint, Rosemary, Sage, Sandalwood, St. John's Wort, Solomon's Seal, Star Anise, Thyme, Valerian, Vervain, Yarrow, White Rose, White Violet, Wormwood |
| Sleep | Agrimony, Bergamot, Bluebell, Catnip, Chamomile, Dandelion, Dill, Heather, Jasmine, Lady's Mantle, Lavender, Mandrake, Marjoram, Mugwort, Nutmeg, Passionflower, Rosemary, Thyme, Valerian, Vervain, Violet |
| Strength | Allspice, Angelica, Bamboo, Basil, Broom, Carnation, Catnip, Comfrey, Cinnamon, Fennel, Feverfew, Galangal, Garlic, Geranium, Honeysuckle, Horehound, Lavender, Mistletoe, Monkshood, Mugwort, Mustard, Myrrh, Nettle, Peppermint, Rose, Saffron, Sage, Spearmint, Sunflower, Thistle, Thyme, Vanilla, Yarrow |
| Stress (relief) | Angelica, Aster, Basil, Bergamot, Catnip, Chamomile, Dandelion, Dill, Fennel, Foxglove, Geranium, Honeysuckle, Hyacinth, Jasmine, Lavender, Lemon Balm, Marjoram, Nettle, Peppermint, Sage, Strawberry, Thyme, Valerian, Vanilla, Vervain, Violet, Wormwood |
| Transformation | Flax, Frankincense, Grape, Ivy, Marigold, Myrrh, Violet, Wormwood |
| Willpower | Allspice, Dill, Dragon's Blood, Heliotrope, Iris, Lily, Rosemary, St. John's Wort. |
| Wisdom | Bamboo, Broom, Dill, Geranium, Hyacinth, Iris, Rose, Rosemary, Rue, Sage, Solomon's Seal, Sunflower |

# Herbs

|  |  |
|---|---|
|  |  |
|  |  |
|  |  |
|  |  |
|  |  |
|  |  |
|  |  |
|  |  |
|  |  |
|  |  |
|  |  |
|  |  |

# Monthly Moons

You'll find the following correspondences for the full moons in this order:
Alternate Moon Names / Nature Spirits / Herbs / Colours / Flowers /
Scents /Stones / Animals / Deities

|  | |
|---|---|
| **January**<br>*Wolf Moon* | *Quiet Moon, Snow Moon, Cold Moon, Moon of Little Winter* Gnomes, Brownies / Marjoram, Holy Thistle, Nuts & Cones / Brilliant White, Blue Violet, Black / Musk / Garnet, Onyx, Jet, Chrysoprase / Birch Tree / Fox, Coyote / Freyja, Inanna, Sarasvati, Hera, Ch'ang-O, Sinn |
| | |
| **February**<br>*Ice Moon* | *Storm Moon, Horning Moon, Hunger Moon, Wild Moon, Big Winter Moon* / House Faeries / Balm of Gilead, Hyssop, Myrrh, Sage / Light Blue, Violet / Primrose / Wisteria, Heliotrope / Amethyst, Jasper / Rowan, Laurel, Cedar / Otter, Unicorn / Brigid, Juno, Kuan, Diana, Demeter, Persephone, Aphrodite. |
| | |
| **March**<br>*Storm Moon* | *Seed Moon, Plow Moon, Worm Moon, Sap Moon, Moon of Winds* / Mer-People, Air & Water beings / Broom, High John, Irish Moss / Pale Green, Red-Violet / Daffodil, Violet / Honeysuckle, Apple Blossom / Aquamarine, Bloodstone / Alder, Dogwood / Cougar, Hedgehog, Boar / Black Isis, the Morrigan, Hecate, Cybele, Astarte, Athene, Minerva, Artemis, Luna |
| | |

# Monthly Moons

You'll find the following correspondences for the full moons in this order:
Alternate Moon Names / Nature Spirits / Herbs / Colours / Flowers /
Scents /Stones / Animals / Deities

| April **Hare Moon** | *Growing Moon, Planting Moon, Pink Moon* / Plant Faeries / Basil, Chives, Dragon Blood, Geranium, Thistle / Crimson Red, Gold / Daisy, Sweetpea / Pine, Bay, Bergamot, Patchouli / Ruby, Garnet, Sard / Pine, Bay, Hazel / Bear, Wolf / Kali, Hathor, Anahita, Ceres, Ishta, Venus, Bast |
|---|---|
| | |
| May **Flower Moon** | *Hare moon, Merry Moon, Bright Moon, Dyad Moon* / Faeries, Elves / Elder, Mint, Rose, Mugwort, Thyme, Yarrow / Green, Brown, Pink / Lily of the Valley, Foxglove, Rose, Broom / Rose, Sandalwood / Emerald, Malachite, Amber, Carnelian / Hawthorn / Cats, Lynx, Leopard / Bast, Venus, Aphrodite, Maia, Diana, Artemis, Pan, Horned God |
| | |
| June **Mead Moon** | *Lovers' Moon, Moon of Horses, Honey Moon, Strawberry Moon, Rose Moon* / Sylphs, Zephyrs / Meadowsweet, Vervain, Dog Grass, Parsley, Mosses / Orange, Golden-Green, Gold / Lavender, Orchid, Yarrow / Lily of the Valley, Lavender / Topaz, Agate, Alexandrite, Fluorite / Monkey, Butterfly, Frog, Toad / Isis, Neith, Green Man, Cerridwen, Bendis, Ishtar |
| | |

# Monthly Moons

| | |
|---|---|
| **July**<br>*Hay Moon* | *Wort Moon, Blessing Moon, Buck Moon, Thunder Moon* / Hobgoblins, Crop Faeries / Honeysuckle, Lemon Balm, Hyssop / Silver, Blue-Gray / Lotus, Water Lily, Jasmine / Orris, Frankincense / Peal, Moonstone, White Agate / Crab, Turtle, Dolphin, Whale / Khepera, Athene, Juno, Hel, Holda, Cerridwen, Nephthys, Venus |
| | |
| **August**<br>*Corn Moon* | *Barley Moon, Harvest Moon, Dispute Moon* / Dryads / Chamomile, St. John's Wort, Bay, Angelica, Fennel, Rue, Orange / Yellow, Gold / Sunflower, Marigold / Frankincense, Heliotrope / Cat's Eye, Carnelian, Jasper, Fire Agate / Lion, Phoenix, Sphinx, Dragon / Ganesha, Thoth, Hathor, Diana, Hecate, Nemesis |
| | |
| **September**<br>*Harvest Moon* | *Wine Moon, Singing Moon, Sturgeon Moon, Moon When Deer Paw the Earth* / Trooping Faeries / Fennel, Rye, Wheat, Valerian, Skullcap / Brown, Yellow-Green, Yellow / Narcissus, Lily / Gardenia, Bergamot / Peridot, Chrysolite, Citrine / Snake, Jackal / Demeter, Ceres, Isis, Nephthys, Freyja, Ch'ang-O, Thoth |
| | |
| **October**<br>*Blood Moon* | *Harvest Moon, Shedding Moon, Falling Leaf Moon, Ten Colds Moon* / Frost & Plant Faeries / Pennyroyal, Thyme, Catnip, Angelica, Burdock / Dark Blue-Green / Calendula, Marigold / Strawberry, Apple Blossom, Cherry / Opal, Tourmaline, Beryl, Turquoise / Stag, Jackal, Elephant, Ram, Scorpion / Ishtar, Astarte, Demeter, Kore, Lakshmi, Horned God, Belili, Hathor |
| | |

# Monthly Moons

| November | Dark Moon, Fog Moon, Beaver Moon, Mourning Moon, Mad Moon, Moon of Storms / Subterranean Faeries / Verbena, Betony, Borage, Blessed Thistle / Gray, Sea-Green / Blooming Cacti, Chrysanthemum / Cedar, Cherry Blossoms, Hyacinth, Narcissus, Peppermint, Lemon / Topaz, Lapis Lazuli / Unicorn, Scorpion, Crocodile, Jackal / Kali, Black Isis, Hecate, Bast, Osiris, Sarasvati, Lakshmi, Skadi, Mawu |
|---|---|
| *Snow Moon* | |
| | |
| **December** | Oak Moon, Wolf Moon, Big Winter Moon, Long Night's Moon / Snow, Storm & Winter Tre Faeries / Holly, English Ivy, Fir, Mistletoe / Blood Red, White, Black / Holly, Poinsettia, Christmas Cactus / Violet, Patchouli, Frankincense, Myrrh, Lilac / Serpentine, Peridot / Mouse, Deer, Horse, Bear / Hathor, Hecate, Neith, Athene, Minerva, Ixchel, Osiris, Norns, Fates |
| *Cold Moon* | |
| | |
| **Blue Moon** | Moon of the Dead, Hunting Moon, Ancestor Moon / Banshees, Messengers between Worlds / Ginger, Hops, Wormwood, Hyssop, Patchouli, Mugwort, Nutmeg, Star Anise / Black, White, Purple / White lily, Dahlia, Chrysanthemum / Rosemary, Dragons Blood, Lilac, Pine, Wisteria / Obsidian, Onyx, Apache Tear / Bat, Wolf, Dog, Snake / Cybele, Circe, Hel, Nephthys, Cerridwen, Horned God, Caillech, Freyja, Holda |
| *The Second Full Moon in any Moon Cycle* | |
| | |

# Moon Phases

### New Moon
*Day 0, Day 29.5*

-deconstructive magic
-banishing
-curses
-divination
-good for new starts in life, love, career

### Full Moon
*Day 13-15*

-protection/banishing
-cleansing
-charging
-healing
-hearts desire

### Waxing Crescent
*Day 3*

-putting together plans
-constructive magic
-success
-positive magic

### Waning Gibbous
*Day 18*

-cleansing negativity
-undoing curses/hexes
-getting rid of energies

### First Quarter
*Day 7*

-growth
-strength
-developing/receiving love

### Last Quarter
*Day 21*

-breaking bad habits
-ridding of negativity (mental/physical)
-cleansing

### Waxing Gibbous
*Day 11*

-attraction
-success
-health
-motivation
-final stages of planning

### Waning Crescent
*Day 25*

-meditation
-balancing
-ridding of illness

# Sabbats

| | |
|---|---|
| **Samhain** | **Focus:** ancestors, beginnings, change, death, preservation, wisdom, other worlds. **Deities:** Cerridwen, Demeter, Hecate, Hel, Inanna, Ishtar, Isis, Kali, the Morrigan, Persephone, Rhiannon. Cernunnos, Hades, the Horned God, Janus, Osiris, Taranis. **Colours:** Black, Brown, Grey, Orange, Yellow, Silver. **Herbs:** Broom, Garlic, Mugwort, Myrrh, Rosemary, Sage, Wormwood, Yarrow. **Crystals:** Carnelian, Jet, Moonstone, Obsidian, Onyx, Iron, Silver. **Totems:** Black Cats, Owls, Ravens, Spiders. **Oils:** Cinnamon, Clove, Myrrh, Pine Needles, Honey. **Foods:** Apple, Pumpkin, Raw & Roasted Nuts. **Drinks:** Apple Cider. **Symbols:** Cauldron, Besom, Mask |
| | |
| **Yule** | **Focus:** birth, beginnings, cycles, eternity, rebirth, silence, sleep, gratitude **Deities:** Amatseru, Baba Yaga, Befana, Caillech, Demeter, Ceres, Holda, Skadi, Bacchus, Hodhr, Saturn, Krampus **Colours:** Green, Gold, Red, White. **Herbs:** Cardamom, Cinnamon, Cloves, Evergreens, Ivy, Mistletoe, Nutmeg, Peppermint, Rosemary, Sage, Saffron **Crystals:** Onyx, Tanzanite, Turquoise **Totems:** Bear, Cows, Reindeer, Horse, Pigs, Raven,. **Oils:** Cardamom, Cinnamon, Clove, Evergreens, Frankincense, Myrrh, Wood Smoke **Foods:** Büche do Noel, Fruitcake, Scalloped/Mashed/Roasted/Au Gratin Vegetables **Drinks:** Eggnog, Rum, Hot Chocolate, Hot Toddy, Mulled Wine, Tea **Symbols:** Cauldron, Darkness, Evergreens, Light, Trees, Wreaths, Yule Log |
| | |
| **Imbolc** | **Focus:** preparation, patience, awakening, newness, cleansing, seeds, fertility. **Deities:** Brigid, Aohrodite, Diana, Athena, Danu, Gaia, Juno, Selene, Vesta, Bragi, Cupid, Eros. **Colours:** Light Green, Pink, White, Yellow **Herbs:** Angelica, Basil, Blackberry/Bramble, Cinnamon, Grain, Reed, Wormwood. **Crystals:** Amethyst, Turqupise. **Totems:** Cow, Dragon, Groundhog, Lark, Robin, Sheep, Snake, Swan. **Oils:** Cedar, Peppermint, Basil, Cinnamon. **Foods:** Dried Fruits, Grains, Potatoes, Cheese, Salted Meats, Nuts, Eggs **Drinks:** Dairy Products, Ale, Mead, Cider **Symbols:** Brigids Cross, Corn Dollies, Candles, Cauldron, Broom |
| | |
| **Ostara** | **Focus:** balance, birth, change, fertility, light, rebirth, rejuvenation, renewal **Deities:** Aphrodite, Eos, Eostre, Epona, Flora, Freya, Gaia, Maia, Persephone, Vila, Cernunnos, the Dagda, Eros, the Green Man, Mabon, Osiris, Pan, Thor **Colours:** Green, Light Blue, Pink, Silver, Violet, White, Yellow **Herbs:** Broom, High John Root, Irish Moss, Lemon Grass **Crystals:** Agate, Aquamarine, Bloodstone **Totems:** Bees, Boar, Butterflies, Chicks, Hedgehog, Horse, Phoenix, Rabbit, Ram, Robin. **Oils:** Apple Blossom, Crocus, Daffodil, Daisy, Honeysuckle, Jasmine, Lilac, Rose, Rain **Foods:** Asparagus, Dill, Eggs, Honey, Lamb, Lettuce, Seafood. **Drinks:** Mead. **Symbols:** Basket, Eggs, Hare, Seeds. |
| | |

| Beltane | Focus: abundance, creation, fertility, growth, psychic ability, union. Deities: Aphrodite, Artemis, Astarte, Danu, Diana, Flora, Freya, Horae, Venus, Apollo, Baldur, Bel, Cernunnos, Horned God, Odin, Pan, Pluto, Ra Colours: Brown, Green, Pink, White, Yellow Herbs: Lemon, Mint, Mugwort, Woodruff Crystals: Bloodstone, Emerald, Rose Quartz Totems: Bees, Cow, Dove, Frog, Rabbit Oils: Frankincense, Jasmine, Lemon, Mint, Pine, Rose, Ylang-Ylang Foods: Honey, Light Cakes Drinks: Lemonade, May Wine. Symbols: Flowers, Maypole. |
|---|---|
|  |  |
| Litha | Focus: abundance, cleansing, divination, fire, growth, love, motherhood, power, warmth. Deities: Amaunet, Anuket, Aphrodite, Artemis, Aphrodite, Athena, Bast, Brigid, Cerridwen, Eos, Epona, Frigga, Gaia, Hathor, Hera, Hestia, Ishtar, Inanna, Rhiannon, Juno, Sul, Vesta, Apollo, Balder, Belinos, Helios, Hoder, Janus, Jupiter, Lugh, Odin, Prometheus, Ra, Aol, Thor, Vishnu, Zeus Colours: Gold, Green, Orange, Red, White, Yellow Herbs: Cinnamon, Foxglove, Mistletoe, Mugwort, Rosemary, St. Johns Wort, Vervain, Yarrow Crystals: Carnelian, Citrine, Diamond, Emerald, Jade, Peridot, Tiger's Eye Totems: Bees, Bull, Butterflies, Cow, Hawks, Eagles, Horse, Summer Birds Oils: Cinnamon, Heliotrope, Lavender, Lemon, Mown Grass, Orange, Peppermint, Pine, Rose, Sandalwood Foods: Berries, Cheese, Grapes, Honey, Lemons, Oranges, Peaches, Pears, Pine Nuts, Spinach, Summer Squash, Sunflower Seeds Drinks: Ale, Lemonade, Mead, Milk, Mint Tea, Sun Tea, Wine. Symbols: Bonfire, Cauldron, Faeries, Roses, Sacred Wells, Sun Wheel, Spinning Wheels, Spirals, Wand |
|  |  |
| Lammas | Focus: gratitude, abundance, blessings, harvest, celebration, reflection, sacrifice. Deities: Isis, Dryads, Demeter, Kore, Nemesis, Ops, Hathor, Hecate, Diana, Danu, Artemis, Osiris, Lugh, Ganesha, Thor, Vulcan, Thoth, Loki, Apollo Colours: Yellow, Brown, Gold, Green Herbs: Blackberry, Bilberry, Allspice, Basil, Rosemary, Garlic, Bay, Fennel Crystals: Citrine, Topaz, Carnelian, Onyx, Quartz Totems: Lion, Stag, Eagle, Dog, Squirrel, Oils: Cinnamon, Apple, Blackberry, Marigold, Patchouli Foods: Apples, Corn, Bread, Squash, Grains, Nuts, Berries, Potatoes Drinks: Wine, Mead, Apple Cider Symbols: Corn Dolly, Rowan Cross, Cornucopia, Pentacle |
|  |  |
| Mabon | Focus: Accomplishment, Balance, Death, Gratitude, Healing, Preparation, Success Deities: Demeter, Epona, Inanna, Juno, Minerva, the Muses, Persephone, Apollo, Dionysus, the Green Man, Hermes, Jupiter, Mabon, Thor, Thoth, Vulcan Colours: Brown, Green, Orange, Red, Yellow Herbs: Acorns, Bay, Echinacea, Hyssop, Ivy, Myrrh, Sage, Solomon's Seal, Tobacco, Yarrow Crystals: Amber, Golden Topaz, Hematite, Totems: Blackbird, Eagle, Goose, Horses, Owl, Salmon, Squirrels, Stag, Oils: Aloe, Cinnamon, Cedar, SLove, Frankincense, Myrrh, Pine Foods: Apple, Barley, Bread, Carrots, Corn, Gourds, Melons, Nuts, Oats, Onions, Rye, Wheat Drinks: Beer, Cider, Mead, Water, Wine Symbols: Cornucopia, Scarecrow, Basket, Garlands, Wreaths, Scythes, Bollines, Sickles |
|  |  |

# Tarot Key
## The Suits

| | |
|---|---|
| **Wands**<br><br>*Your Interpretations:* | Element: Fire<br>**Key Words:** Drive, Creativity, Ambitious, Goals, Motivation, Vision, Energy, Competition, Passion, Passionate, Restless, Egotism, Pride, Hot-Tempered<br><br>When a spread is dominated by the **Wands** suit, it indicates that the situation is one that resides mostly in your mind. Something that is weighing on your mind or that you can't stop thinking about. |
| **Cups**<br><br>*Your Interpretations:* | Element: Water<br>**Key Words:** Emotion, Human Contact, Relationships, Family, Feelings, Desires, Love, Friendship, Connection, Intuition, Sensual Pleasure, Lust, Heart-Overruling-Head<br><br>When a spread is dominated by the **Cups** suit, it indicates that the situation is one that deals with your heart and emotions. Toying with them or something you feel very strongly about. |
| **Swords**<br><br>*Your Interpretations:* | Element: Air<br>**Key Words:** Intellect, Wisdom, Thought, The Mind, Connection, Expression, Information, Wisdom, Know-It-All, Head Overruling-Heart.<br><br>When a spread is dominated by the **Swords** suit, it indicates that the situation tends to revolve around change and conflict. This generally does not indicate a harmonious situation, as these are usually ones that cause distress. |
| **Pentacles**<br><br>*Your Interpretations:* | Element: Earth<br>**Key Words:** Money, Abundance, Substance, Career, Home, Health, Tangible, Reality, Stability, Grounding, Obsession, Possession, Control.<br><br>When a spread is dominated by the **Pentacles** suit, it indicates that the situation revolves around material aspects, or ones that involve property, home, career, or income. |

# Tarot Key
## Minor Arcana

|  | Wands | Cups | Swords | Pentacles |
|---|---|---|---|---|
| **Ace** | New (creative) idea, birth, fertile time | New relationship, new appreciation for current relationship | Clarity, new understanding, honesty | New job, prosperity, income, starting fresh |
|  |  |  |  |  |
| **Two** | Right direction, focused, determined, | Sometimes known as the true lovers card, love, establishing a bond, harmony, understanding | Denial, blocked feelings, being calm but unavailable, unwilling to make a choice | Going with the flow, balancing, dealing with change well, confidence |
|  |  |  |  |  |
| **Three** | Rely on yourself, vision the future, support yourself | Friendship, celebration, abundant feelings, community giving, celebrations | Being self aware will bring you a clear head, betrayal, heartbreak, feeling let down | Teamwork, relying on those around you, strategy, obsessed with detail |
|  |  |  |  |  |
| **Four** | Completion, celebration, mark the occasion , party | Self-concerned, doubt, questioning, lack of self-appreciation | Retreat, relaxing, staying calm in unknown situations | Limited viewpoint, possessive, feeling its mine |
|  |  |  |  |  |

# Tarot Key
## Minor Arcana

| | Wands | Cups | Swords | Pentacles |
|---|---|---|---|---|
| **Five** | Distress, frustration, competition, challenges, scattered | Disappointment, loss, emotionally confused, emotional resistance | Finding & accepting limitations, hollow victory, defeat, selfish thinking | Worry, loss, illness, victim mentality, rejection, something is missing |
| | | | | |
| **Six** | Overcoming adversity, coming out of darkness, victory, pride | Innocence, nostalgia, childhood memories/friends, sentimental, inner child | Leaving the past behind, new perspective, a new positive outlook on life | Bountiful harvest, fruits of your labor, generosity (form you or to you), gifts |
| | | | | |
| **Seven** | Defensive, confident, saying no, struggling with opposition | Too many options, disorganised, fantasizing the future, high expectations, wishful thinking | Blind to the truth, dishonesty, deception, keeping a secret (from others or yourself) | Evaluating your progress, getting results, planning next moves, taking a small break |
| | | | | |
| **Eight** | Rushing ahead, movement, developments, swift action | Change of direction, moving on, nothing left in current situation, realizing emotional truths | Feeling trapped, unable to get out without being incredibly hurt, bound, powerless, victim | Honing your craft, mastery, training, discipline and diligence in work, detail oriented |
| | | | | |

# Tarot Key
## Minor Arcana

Decan = 10 days

| | Wands | Cups | Swords | Pentacles |
|---|---|---|---|---|
| **Nine** | Vulnerable, cautious, remembering past issues, suspicious, proactively defensive | Wish card, dreams coming true, achieving greatest desires | Guilt, worrying about past transgressions, obsessed with "if only"'s, darkest time before the dawn | Accomplishments, material/financial security, having situational control |
| | | | | |
| **Ten** | Burden, overextending yourself, workhorse, big workload | Joy, radiating energy, peace, attaining loves ideals, commitment | Rock bottom, being melodramatic, playing the victim, exaggerating self-pity | Experiencing the good things in life, happy family life and home, success |
| | | | | |
| **Page** | Messenger/messages, childlike exuberance, fresh ideas, take a chance | Youthful energy, young lover, young love, flirtatious, romantic energy | Logical, reasonable, ready for action, wisdom from experience, refreshingly honest | Practical approach, realistic goals, setting plans in motion, new projects |
| | | | | |
| **Knight** | Daring, passionate, over exaggerates and over promises, adventurous but restless. Last decan of Cancer, first two decans of Leo | Knight in shining armour, emotional rescue, in love with love, many sentiments Last decan of Libra, first two decan of Scorpio | Self-assured, quick action, charging ahead, impatient, cut off from emotion Last decan of Capricorn, first two decans of Aquarius | Hardworking, responsible, passionless effort, working for the sake of working Last decan of Aries, first two decans of Taurus |
| | | | | |

161

# Tarot Key
## Minor Arcana

Decan = 10 days

| | Wands | Cups | Swords | Pentacles |
|---|---|---|---|---|
| **Queen** | Know what you want & where you're going, attractive, magnetic, leader, optimistic<br>Last decan of Pisces, first two decans of Aries | Prioritizing emotional understanding, unconditional love, empathy, emotional involvement.<br>Last decan of Gemini, first two decans of Cancer | Problem solving, up-front and honest, realistic plans, judgemental, fast thinker<br>Last decan of Virgo, first two decans of Libra | Reliability, loyal, home-loving, lover of animals & children, resourceful.<br>Last decan of Sagittarius, first two decans of Capricorn |
| | | | | |
| **King** | Bold, dramatic, inspiring, leader, art mastery, charismatic, male authority figure.<br>Last decan of Scorpio, first two decans of Sagittarius | Emotional maturity and security, keeping emotionally calm, balancing atmosphere<br>Last decan of Aquarius, first two decans of Pisces | Direct, assertive, objective outlook, cutting through mental confusion.<br>Last decan of Taurus, first two decans of Gemini | Enterprises, made it to the top, responsible, practical, stabilizing<br>Last decan of Leo, first two decans of Virgo |
| | | | | |

# Tarot Key
## Major Arcana

| | | |
|---|---|---|
| **The Fool (0)** <br> *Uranus* | Impulsive, childlike, jumping in, spontaneous, new beginnings. | |
| **The Magician (1)** <br> *Mercury* | All of the tools to achieve, goal focused, knowledge. | |
| **The High Priestess (2)** <br> *Moon* | Secrets (revealed), seeing beyond what's in front of you, the unknown. | |
| **The Empress (3)** <br> *Venus* | Action, development, harmony with the natural world, creative | |
| **The Emperor (4)** <br> *Aries* | Power, authority figure, leadership, structure thought | |
| **The Hierophant (5)** *Taurus* | Teacher, teaching, knowledge seeker. | |
| **The Lovers (6)** <br> *Gemini* | What is love, relationships of all kinds, union, commitment | |
| **The Chariot (7)** <br> *Cancer* | Diligence, willpower, things happening at fast pace | |
| **Strength (8)** <br> *Leo* | Courage, inner strength, self-awareness | |
| **The Hermit (9)** <br> *Virgo* | Withdrawing, spending time alone, self-searching | |
| **Wheel of Fortune (10)** <br> *Jupiter* | Fate, inevitability, destiny, timing, change is coming | |

# Tarot Key
## Major Arcana

| | | |
|---|---|---|
| **Justice (11)**<br>*Libra* | Fairness, balancing, accepting the truth | |
| **The Hanged Man (12)**<br>*Neptune* | Being in limbo, paradox, being at a crossroads, taking a step back | |
| **Death (13)**<br>*Scorpio* | New beginnings, change, transformation | |
| **Temperance (14)**<br>*Sagittarius* | Self-control, harmony, understanding, balancing opposing factors | |
| **The Devil (15)**<br>*Capricorn* | Obsession, materialism, temptation, addiction, negative thoughts | |
| **The Tower (16)**<br>*Mars* | Disruption, sudden unexpected change, unwelcomed change, chaos | |
| **The Star (17)**<br>*Aquarius* | Self-expression, visionary progress, inspiration, seeing the light in the dark | |
| **The Moon (18)**<br>*Pisces* | Intuition, shadow self, worried, apprehensive, blind to the truth | |
| **The Sun (19)**<br>*Sun* | Shining down, happiness, warmth in your soul, sharing joy | |
| **Judgement (20)**<br>*Pluto* | Forgiveness (of others & the self,) acceptance, taking account, no blame | |
| **The World (21)**<br>*Saturn* | Completion, fulfilment, achievement, happiness, accomplishment, acceptance | |

# Zodiacs

Before we get into the correspondences around each Zodiac season, I want to point out a few things when it comes to the dates and timing of each one. There is no "one and done" timeframe for the Zodiac signs. Due to the extra 25% of a day we get each year, and the whole extra day on Leap Years, the start and end times of each season can differ by a day or two, year to year. As well, the sun does not move on a calendar or change signs at midnight, so 99.9% of the time, the signs will end and start on the same day as the sign previous to them.

This means that if you were born really early on the last day of Libra, and someone else was born late on the first day of Scorpio, it is possible you will have the same birth **date** but different sun signs. Your birth **time**, and your birth **location** are only part of the requirements for figuring out your accurate sun sign, especially if your birth date is at the end or beginning of a zodiac season.

Simple googling "sun times for entering zodiacs for (your location)" will give you an accurate timeframe year to year. The dates below include several of the variations of dates for each sign.

| | |
|---|---|
| **Aries**<br><br>Mar 21/24 –<br>Apr 18/21<br><br> | Element: Fire. **Status:** Cardinal. **Day:** Tuesday. **Planet:** Mars, Sun. **Colours:** Scarlett, White, Pink. **Chakras:** Root, Solar Plexus, Brow. **Seasons:** Spring, Summer. **Celebration:** Spring Equinox **Crystals:** Bloodstone, Diamond, Ruby, Red Jasper, Garnet. **Herbs:** Geranium, Sage, Tiger Lily, Thistle, Rose. **Deities:** Isis, Athena, Shiva, Mars, Minerva. **Tarot:** The Emperor. **Intentions & Powerflow:** Ambition, Beginnings, Courage, Desires, Growth, Leadership, Lust, Needs, Obstacles, Passion, Pregnancy, Sexuality, Warmth |
| | |
| **Taurus**<br><br>Apr 21/23 –<br>May 20/24<br><br> | Element: Earth. **Status:** Fixed **Day:** Friday **Planet:** Earth, Venus **Colours:** Red, Orange, Brown, Indigo **Chakras:** Root, Heart, Throat **Season:** Spring **Crystals:** Sapphire, Turquoise, Jade, Emerald, Topaz. **Herbs:** Burdock, Elder, Vervain, Violet, Wild Rose, Clover. **Deities:** Osiris, Apis, Asar, Hera, Venus **Tarot:** The Empress, The Hierophant, Pentacles **Intentions & Powerflow:** Affection, Comfort, Dedication, Endurance, Grounding, Intuit on, Life, Love, Lust, the Mind, Money, Organize, Patience, Protection, the Sense, Stability, Wealth |
| | |

# Zodiacs

| | |
|---|---|
| **Gemini**<br><br>May 22/26–<br>June 18–21<br><br>♊ | **Element**: Air. **Status**: Mutable. **Day**: Wednesday **Planet**: Mercury, Uranus, **Colours**: White, Yellow, Orange. **Chakras**: Heart, Throat. **Season**: Summer **Crystals**: Moss Agate, Onyx, Jade, Topaz, Diamond. **Herbs**: Orchid, Dill, Gladioli, Parsley, Iris, Snapdragon. **Deities**: Bast & Sekhmet, Castor & Pollux, Frey & Freyja, Janus. **Tarot**: The Magician, The Lovers **Intentions & Powerflow**: Adaptability, Balance, Change, Communication, Creativity, Emotions, Intelligence, Knowledge, Relationships, Truth |
| | |
| **Cancer**<br><br>June 19/22–<br>July 20/23<br><br>♋ | **Element**: Water. **Status**: Cardinal. **Day**: Monday. **Planet**: Moon, Pluto, Sun **Colours**: Amber, White, Silver **Chakras**: Sacral, Solar Plexus, Heart. **Season**: Summer. **Celebration**: Midsummer's Eve. **Crystals**: Moonstone, Cats Eye, Pearl, Emerald, Amber. **Herbs**: Passion Flower, Balm, Comfrey, Water Lily. **Deities**: Khapera, Mercury, Apollo. **Tarot**: The High Priestess, The Chariot **Intentions & Powerflow**: Beginnings, Change, Connections, Conscious & Sub Consciousness, Emotions, Family, the Home, Imagination, Intuition, Love, Magic, Nurture, Protection, Psychic Ability, Romance, Shyness, Support, Sympathy |
| | |
| **Leo**<br><br>July 22/24–<br>Aug 21–23<br><br>♌ | **Element**: Fire. **Status**: Fixed. **Day**: Sunday. **Planet**: Sun **Colours**: Amber, White, Silver **Chakras**: Solar Plexus, Heart. **Season**: Summer. **Crystals**: Amber, Ruby, Diamond, Golden Topaz. **Herbs**: Chamomile, Saffron, Sunflower, Marigold **Deities**: Horus, Sekhmet, Demeter, Vishnu, Venus **Tarot**: Strength, The Sun, Wands **Intentions & Powerflow**: Action, Affection, Ambition, Communication, Confidence, Courage, Determination, Friendship, Growth, Guardian, Guidance, Leadership, Light, Love, Loyalty, Animal Magic, Passion, Pleasure, Pride, Romance, Strength, Warmth, Willpower |
| | |
| **Virgo**<br><br>Aug 22–24–<br>Sept 20–22<br><br>♍ | **Element**: Earth **Status**: Mutable **Day**: Wednesday **Planet**: Earth, Mercury. **Colours**: Moss Green, Mauve, Rose, Pink **Chakras**: Sacral, Solar Plexus, Throat **Season**: Summer. **Crystals**: Jade, Carnelian, Diamond, Jasper, Aquamarine, Peridot **Herbs**: Lily, Narcissus, Rosemary, Snowdrop, Silver Root **Deities**: Hera, Isis, Adonis, Ceres **Tarot**: The Magician, The Hermit **Intentions & Powerflow**: Abundance, Beginnings, Cycles, Destiny, Endings, Grounding, Independence, Intuition, Love, Organize, Purification, Success, Well-Being |
| | |

# Zodiacs

| Libra<br><br>Sept 21/23–<br>Oct 20/22<br><br> | Element: Air. Status: Cardinal Day: Friday Planet: Saturn, Venus, Colours: Emerald Green Royal Blue, Black Chakras: Sacral, Heart Season: Autumn Crystals: Lapis Lazuli, Jade, Opal, Emerald. Herbs: Violet, Yarrow, White Rose. Deities: Maat, Ma, Themis, Yama, Vulcan. Tarot: Justice, Empress Intentions & Powerflow: Attract, Balance, Business, Community, Cooperation, Fairness, Grace, Harmony, Justice, Love, Romance, Sensitivity, Sympathy, Unity |
|---|---|
| | |
| Scorpio<br><br>Oct 21/23–<br>Nov 19/21<br><br> | Element: Water. Status: Fixed. Day: Tuesday, Planet: Mars, Pluto Colours: Black, Blue, Purple, Crimson Chakras: Root, Sacral. Season: Autumn. Crystals: Aquamarine, Ruby, Topaz, Jet. Herbs: Chrysanthemum, Pine, Rosemary, Vanilla Deities: Hecate, Hel, Isis, Persephone, Anubis, Mars, Pluto. Tarot: Death, Swords Intentions & Powerflow: Authority, Change, Clairvoyance, Control, Darkness, Death, Desire, Emotions, Energy, Healing, Jealousy, Loyalty, Lust, the Underworld, Passion, Power, Psychic Ability, Rebirth, Revenge, Spirituality, Trust, Willpower. |
| | |
| Sag.<br><br>Nov 20/22–<br>Dec 19/21<br><br> | Element: Fire. Status: Mutable Day: Thursday. Planet: Jupiter Colours: Red, Crimson, Darker Shades Chakras: Root, Solar Plexus, Brow. Season: Autumn Celebration: Winter Solstice Crystals: Sapphire, Amethyst, Diamond, Golden Topaz. Herbs: Carnation, Pink Clover, Rush, Sage, Wildflower Deities: Nepthys, Apollo, Artemis, Vishnu, Diana Tarot: Temperance, Wheel of Fortune Intentions & Powerflow: Beauty, Consciousness, Dream Work, Enlightenment, Fear, Freedom, Growth, Honesty, Independence, Intuition, Knowledge, Magic, Prophecy, Self-Work, Sexuality, Travel, Truth, Unity |
| | |
| Virgo<br><br>Aug 22-24–<br>Sept 20-22<br><br> | Element: Earth Status: Mutable Day: Wednesday Planet: Earth, Mercury. Colours: Moss Green, Mauve, Rose, Pink Chakras: Sacral, Solar Plexus, Throat Season: Summer. Crystals: Jade, Carnelian, Diamond, Jasper, Aquamarine, Peridot Herbs: Lily, Narcissus, Rosemary, Snowdrop, Silver Root Deities: Hera, Isis, Adonis, Ceres Tarot: The Hermit Intentions & Powerflow: Abundance, Beginnings, Cycles, Destiny, Endings, Grounding, Independence, Intuition, Love, Organize, Purification, Success, Well-Being |

# Zodiacs

| Capr. | |
|---|---|
| Dec 20/23– Jan 18/20  | **Element:** Earth **Status:** Cardinal **Day:** Thursday **Planet:** Earth, Saturn **Colour:** Gray, Dark, Brown, Indigo, Black **Celebration:** Winter Solstice: **Chakras:** Root, Crown **Season:** Winter **Crystals:** Malachite, Onyx, Garnet, Jet, Obsidian, Turquoise. **Herbs:** Belladonna, Hellebore, Rue, Hemlock, Orris Root **Deities:** Set, Pan, Hermes, Vesta, Bacchus. **Tarot:** The Devil **Intentions & Powerflow:** Accomplishment, Ambition, Beginnings, Confidence, Focus, Cycles, Darkness, Death, Determination, Endings, Grounding, Intuition, Love, Manifestation, Omens, Negativity, Obstacles, Patience, Psychic Ability, Responsibility, Stability, Success, Willpower. |
| | |

| Aquar. | |
|---|---|
| Jan 19/21– Feb 16/18  | **Element:** Air. **Status:** Fixed **Day:** Saturday **Planet:** Uranus, Neptune, Saturn **Colours:** Violet, Purple, Sky Blue **Chakras:** Throat, Brow, Crown. **Season:** Winter **Celebration:** Imbolc **Crystals:** Garnet, Amber, Aquamarine, Lapis Lazuli, Malachite **Herbs:** Buttercup, Fennel, Wormwood **Deities:** Nuit, Athena, Juno, Isis, Ea **Tarot:** The Fool, The Star, Cups **Intentions & Powerflow:** Ambition, Charity, Community Compassion, Creativity, Determination, Freedom, Friendship, Healing, Honesty, Integrity, Intuition, Loyalty, Peace, Spirituality, Wisdom |
| | |

| Pisces | |
|---|---|
| Feb 18/20– Mar 19/21  | **Element:** Water **Status:** Mutable **Day:** Thursday. **Planet:** Neptune, Jupiter. **Colours:** Purple, Crimson, Aqua, Lavender **Chakras:** Brow, Crown. **Season:** Winter **Celebration:** Spring Equinox **Crystals:** Amethyst, Pearl, Sapphire, Emerald **Herbs:** Heliotrope, Carnation, Poppy, Sage **Deities:** Anubis, Khepera, Poseidon, Vishnu, Neptune **Tarot:** The Hanged Man, The Moon **Intentions & Powerflow:** Adaptability, Boundaries, Calm, Clarity, Communication, Compassion, Creativity, Death, Emotions, Enchantment, Imagination, Intuition, Justice, Kindness, Psychic Ability, Romance, Sensitivity, Spirituality, Unity. |
| | |

Made in the USA
Middletown, DE
12 November 2020